Praise for
A Year of Blind Dates

When you read *A Year of Blind Dates,* you will no doubt see yourself in Megan and probably relate to more than one of the "dates" she went on. You will laugh as you read, hope along with Megan that she finds Mr. Right, and applaud as she discovers more about the true beauty God has given her, both inside and out."

Shelly Ballestero
Inspirational Beauty Coach and Author of *Beauty by God*

Megan is a first time writer, but you'd never guess it by this book. I smiled at the title, laughed at the stories and even paused to examine the height, width and depth of the love she pursued. You better cherish this book, because if Megan is as personally endearing as her writing, she won't be single long!

Jason Illian
Speaker and Author of *Undressed: The Naked Truth About Love, Sex and Dating*
Former Contestant on *The Bachelorette*

Megan's storytelling and sense of humor kept me laughing through the entire book. It's now on my favorite books list.

Rich Praytor
Comedian and Author

Megan Carson is warm, witty and oh-so brave. *A Year of Blind Dates* is a charming and funny tale of one woman's quest for love.

Trish Ryan
Author of *He Loves Me, He Loves Me Not: A Memoir of Finding Faith, Hope, and Happily Ever After*

Megan Carson's poignant and entertaining story of her year of blind dates is a must-read for singles who are still holding out for true love. A spiritual dramedy . . . you will laugh and cry and ask yourself if you're up for the challenge to uncover your Adam or Eve. This book makes you think and swoon at the same time.

Shirin Taber
Author of *Wanting All the Right Things*

Could you find your perfect match if you dated every eligible bachelor in the county for a year? Take the journey with Megan. *A Year of Blind Dates* is a comfy companion for all those who brave the dating world.

Reba Toney
Author of *The Rating Game*
Morning Show Host on "The Fish," Los Angeles Radio (95.9)

Big hugs to Megan for bravely sharing her fascinating story of surviving a year of blind dates. Not only is she hilarious (I couldn't put it down), but as Megan creatively shares the highs and lows of her dates, she also goes deeper, revealing how her adventures grew her closer to God. Single ladies, don't lose hope—this "Hugs Lady" found love online at age 42 and is now LeAnn Weiss-Rupard! Trust God as you wait . . . and, meanwhile, have a girlfriend party and get ready to laugh as you read this book.

LeAnn Weiss-Rupard
Coauthor of *Hugs for Friends* and Author of *Valentine Promises*

a Year of Blind Dates

a single girl's search for "the one"

megan carson

Regal

From Gospel Light
Ventura, California, U.S.A.

Published by Regal
From Gospel Light
Ventura, California, U.S.A.
www.regalbooks.com
Printed in the U.S.A.

Published in association with Rosenbaum & Associates
Literary Agency, Inc., of Brentwood, Tennessee.

Library of Congress Cataloging-in-Publication Data
Carson, Megan.
A year of blind dates : a single girl's search for "the one" / Megan Carson.
p. cm.
ISBN 978-0-8307-4810-5 (trade paper)
1. Man-woman relationships. 2. Dating (Social customs)—United States.
3. Mate selection. 4. Carson, Megan—Relations with men. I. Title.
HQ801.A3C36 2009
306.73082'0973—dc22
2009032285

1 2 3 4 5 6 7 8 9 10 / 15 14 13 12 11 10 09

Rights for publishing this book outside the U.S.A. or in non-English languages are
administered by Gospel Light Worldwide, an international not-for-profit ministry.
For additional information, please visit www.glww.org, email info@glww.org, or write
to Gospel Light Worldwide, 1957 Eastman Avenue, Ventura, CA 93003, U.S.A.

To Ethel Marshall Carson

By nature you passed down your love for and talent of writing.

I treasure all of your letters and the stories you've shared with me.

To Laura Little

By nurture you taught me to believe in myself.

I treasure the time, love and endless support you've given me.

Contents

Author's Note

· ·

As you will soon read, when I set out on this blind date journey, my wish was to meet a man. Not just any man, but one who knows my God, is gainfully employed, has some manners and understands golf. Is that really too much to ask for? As this journey progressed, I began sharing my stories and bringing them to life in print. Friends and family laughed with me (and at me) as I told them the details of my blind date experiences. In what can only be described as divine intervention, I was given the chance to share my story with a wider audience. The result is this book you're now holding.

As a first-time author, I have chosen to write about what I know and what I have lived. This book is not intended to be a how-to guide for finding the right man (believe me, you don't want my advice), but an intimate, amusing and true tale. Some of my experiences and perspectives may not be spot on for all single women, but I do believe (unfortunately) they resonate with most. Orange County, California, (my dating domain) is a unique place, really unlike anywhere in the world. I know that some of the things I experienced might be exclusive to Orange County; however, my prayer is that all readers can connect with the humanity and authenticity behind my words.

While some men might be egotistical enough to want to be in this book (Penthouse Pete, I am talking to you), most would want nothing to do with it. For that reason, the names, professions and incriminating details about each man have been changed, or slightly altered. Also, as you read, I ask you to keep in mind that severe emotional and mental trauma tends to be an occupational hazard associated with a year of blind dates. This trauma can result in delusional behavior and memory lapses. Consequently, I have taken a few liberties to fill in the informational gaps where my memory has failed me. Some of this story is not entirely accurate; however, I am sad to report, most of it is.

But, you're in luck. I've survived the trauma (and the drama) of it all, and I've lived to tell. Enjoy.

. . . .

Prologue

. . . .

College degree:	☑
Fulfilling job:	☑
Supportive family:	☑
Relationship with God:	☑
Community of friends:	☑
Good looks:	☑
Relationship with a man who loves her *and* her God:	☐

So, why is that last item missing a checkmark? Let me try to explain.

I had my first kiss at the late age of 27. Call it pathetic, strategic, endearing, whatever you like. It's the honest truth. My high-school classmates voted me "Most Likely to Become a Nun." On more than a few lonely nights, I've thought they could be right. I never played Spin the Bottle (wait, what I meant to say is, the bottle never landed on me). No seven minutes in heaven. New Year's Eves were spent passing out high fives and hugs to "friends." Sometimes I wore my "Never Been Kissed" badge with pride, but most of the time I was deeply embarrassed. I cringed at slumber parties when the girl with the Barbie proportions, perfect hair and too much perkiness said, "Okay, everyone share their first kiss story!" I began to dread the day it might actually happen, wondering if perhaps my peak kissing years were behind me. Who wants to admit at 27 that they have never been kissed? What was wrong with me? I had near flawless teeth, nice breath, could tie a cherry stem with my tongue . . . didn't that count for something?

If it was just about the kiss, I could easily make that happen. It couldn't be that hard to find someone to teach me a thing or two. Maybe a dare, or a kissing booth at the Fourth of July fair. I have no doubt—if it was just about the kiss—I could get the job done. But it was about so much more. It was about kissing someone who cared about me . . . someone I wanted to be with. So, instead of resorting to desperate measures, I gave the request to God. As I entered my twenty-seventh year, blowing out the candles on my bite-size brownie sundae in an overpriced Chicago eatery, and with my dear friends Leigh and Amanda at my side, I formed a request that was part wish, part prayer, part reprimand: "God, it's not funny anymore. Can I please have a kiss this year?"

I'd like to think that God appreciated my honest approach. I'd always tried to tell Him exactly how I was feeling, but I was doubtful that this was actually going to happen. Did He even care? I'd been wishing for a man for quite some time, and well, that was one wish that had not come true.

But this time, God delivered. My twenty-seventh year was a memorable one. I went on my first real date. A friendship ensued, then a relationship. Chris and I were set up by his aunt and uncle, who claimed we'd be *perfect* for each other. There was only one slight problem; Chris lived in Colorado, and I lived in California. After our first meeting in California, we dated via texts, emails, phone calls and old-fashioned letters. Our little romance was a great first experience for me; I reveled in the thrill of liking someone who truly, honestly liked me back.

I proudly ditched my "Never Been Kissed" badge late one night on my second trip to Colorado. The backdrop was a moonlit snow-covered field. I wore two layers of winter clothes and a pair of hiking boots—one size too big. Awkward? Yes. Magical? Absolutely.

The relationship lasted about three months, and while I did not truly love Chris, I was heartbroken when it ended. He was my first boyfriend. I was like a sorry 16-year-old trapped in a 27-year-old body. The dream of marrying the first guy I dated (*why else would I have my first boyfriend at 27, unless he was going to be my only boyfriend?*); the return to Singleton when I loved life in Couple-hood; and the reality that I'd have to go through this all over again was crushing. I shut down. I cried a lot, slept less and ate too much. I was grieving the loss of the relationship, but more so, I was grieving the *loss of who I was* in a relationship. I had never met "Megan the Girlfriend," but once I did, I really liked her. I missed her. I wanted her back. I firmly believe that we are created to be in relationship, and I felt like I was out of step being single again.

So what does a grieving, sleep-deprived, wallowing in self-loathing girl do? I joined an online dating service. Late one night I signed up for Match.com. *Note to self: A laptop, glass of wine and a broken heart are not a good combination.* Fifty "winks" later and no face-to-face dates to show for it, I gave up on Match.com. How about eHarmony? Well, I tried that route once before and let's just say it hadn't been pleasant. I came to admit that I really wanted to meet someone the "old-fashioned way," whatever the heck that was.

I remembered recently reading in a magazine about a na-tionwide dating service. This one was for busy professionals whose closest relationship was with their BlackBerry. Okay, so I don't have a BlackBerry, but I do have a busy life as a pro-fessional. They promised driven and successful clientele, well-trained matchmakers, and over 14 first dates in 12 months. This sounded great to me. I had been unsuccessful in finding my own dates; why not let the professionals take a stab at it? I could use all the help I could get. But was I really ready for this? Could I go on several blind dates in one year? Of course I could! All it would take is one good match and I'd be back on Couple Street.

Before I made an official decision, I needed to talk to my dad. When facing a dilemma like this, I always seek out my dad for advice (and make a lengthy pro/con list, of course). He's the kind of man who does not get emotional easily, loves me deeply and can see things very objectively. That is exactly what I needed right now. I pulled out my cell phone and dialed his number.

I began by telling my dad how I was feeling; how—five months post-Chris—I was having a hard time moving on. My half-healed heart was getting in the way of everything. Like a seasoned saleswomen, I pitched the dating service idea to him. He listened and nodded. I continued . . . "I just want to get out there and date, but I feel like I am not meeting anyone I'm remotely interested in. There seems to be men available, just not the type of men I am looking for." *Cue chorus of single women in America.*

Dad was quiet for a minute. Then, after some silence, he began, "Megan, here's what I think . . ." his tone diplomatic (one of his trademark qualities that I have inherited). "I know there are a lot of dating services out there. The kind of man you want to meet is not paying $19.99 a month for some online service. He is willing to spend some significant money to meet the right woman. That's the kind of man you want. It's pretty simple in my eyes. I say go for it." He continued, "I'll make you a deal. I will pay for The World's Best Dating Service, but when you meet Mr. Right via this service, let him know he has to pay me back."

As tempted as I was to take my dad up on his offer, I declined. I could just see myself with *Mr. Right*, "Honey, I am so glad we met," I'd say sweetly, "and I really love you; but if you want to keep seeing me, you owe my dad some serious cash." In the end, I did not envision that would go over very well. And, if I was going to take this risk, I wanted to take it on my own account. So one hot August afternoon, overdressed and sweating bullets, I entered the offices of The World's Best Dating Service.

Meet Megan

When I was born, my parents taped a pink bow to my head while I was still in the hospital. Apparently I looked like a boy when I was first out of the womb (don't all babies look unisex anyway?), and even though they dressed me in plenty of pink, the bow was the exclamation point, saying, "Yes, she's a girl!" This may strike you as typical—most baby girls do wear bows and lots of pink—but I find it ironic because I have never been all that girly. From preschool through eighth grade I sported the dreaded androgynous bowl cut. My childhood memories include many instances when I was mistaken for a boy. Sure, I played with Barbie and Ken (complete with their dream house and Corvette that I purchased at a garage sale with 500 pennies), and I had an awesome sticker collection; but I was still a bit of a tomboy. In an attempt to counteract the short hair and get in touch with my inner girl, I wore dresses every day until second grade. I finally gave those up when I found the monkey bars and realized that dresses inhibited my ability to make the most of recess time.

In elementary school I tried every sport available. One of the rules in the Carson house was if you started an athletic season, you had to finish it. I became very good at playing sports for one or two years. Softball, soccer and gymnastics were dropped when they got too competitive, or in the case of gymnastics, I got too tall. Each summer I was enrolled in junior golf and tennis camp—sports I still play today. But the sport (?) that changed my life was roller-skating. For three years I took skating lessons at Skateway. It was the quintessential '70s-style rink complete with carpet-covered walls, an Icee machine and Rod Stewart's "Do Ya Think I'm Sexy?" looped to play once an hour. Thanks to Skateway, I could do a figure 8 on one leg without falling; but more significantly, I experienced my first crush, with my painfully awkward skating partner Edwin Rogers.

Edwin and I went to the same elementary school. Luckily, we were both in Mrs. Candy's third-grade class. Between the six hours at school and our one-hour skate lesson on Wednesday afternoons, I felt like I spent more time with Edwin than anyone else. Granted, he basically ignored me at school, but at the skating rink he was all mine. He had this full head of feathery hair that moved beautifully when we were skating. Almost every day, Edwin wore a striped shirt and rather short corduroy shorts. He looked adorable when he shoved his pudgy legs into those brown suede stakes. Man, I loved his look. I, too, had a favorite skating outfit: a pink-striped dress (of course, as partners, Edwin and I *had* to match) and white roller skates with pink wheels and laces.

Like a typical third-grade boy, Edwin was interested in GI Joe, playing in the dirt and riding his bike. I got the impression that skating lessons were not his idea, because when it came time to "partner up," he looked at me like he was going to be sick. I did not care. All I wanted was to hold his hand and circle the rink to my favorite Whitney Houston songs. We both suffered from sweaty palms, so we constantly had to readjust our hands while skating, and Edwin was always the first to let go as soon as the last note was played.

I was oblivious to the fact that Edwin was not interested in me until the day he requested a partner change. Apparently, I was too much for him. I was heartbroken and retired from skating as a result. But I did not give up on sports altogether. I realized this was my link to time with the boys, and to this day, I love to watch, play and talk sports. Today, I consider myself an athlete who can compete in everything but not as a superstar at anything. Sports gave me self-confidence, developed a healthy sense of discipline in my life, improved my social skills and nurtured my risk-taking spirit.

Most of junior high passed in a blur (*Thank Goodness!*). Nevertheless, I do remember being teased. A lot. One kid called me an "overstuffed sofa" every time he saw me. Evidently, this was the type of insult used by the high achiever kids, those who were too intelligent to tease me with common phrases like "fatso" or "tub o' lard." This prompted me to lose some baby fat, and I discovered a love of running. Never being the popular kid, I was hoping that high school might be different. I especially hoped that I'd "go out" with someone. Doesn't every girl have her first boyfriend in high school? Well, apparently not everyone. Despite being less than popular with the boys, I made great friends during those four years. Basketball took up most of my time, along with working part-time and youth group. Senior year was great, and I did attend my prom, but only because my older brother convinced one of his friends to take me.

Still single, life moved on. After graduation, I left Orange County to attend Furman University in South Carolina. My older brother was already a student there, but it was still quite risky to move across the country at 18. Immediately, I fell in love with the South and its preppy wardrobe. Crewneck sweaters, polo shirts with popped collars, loafers with plaid skirts, khakis . . . what's not to love? Before long, I was involved in the university's activities committee, campus Bible studies and a sorority. For the first time, I felt great about being me: a confident and sassy co-ed. With confidence came a tremendous desire to date. College is where you meet "The One," right? I had high expectations that I'd be walking down the aisle soon after graduation.

I met plenty of men I thought were good candidates for Mr. Right, but none that would have me. Apparently they did not go for my aggressive (borderline creepy) behavior toward them. I would bake them cookies, send them notes and "randomly" see them at church, at a party or the library. I was trying way too hard, and these sweet Southern boys saw right through my efforts.

By spring of 2000, I had no man and no idea what to do for post-graduation life. Should I go back to California? Set up camp in the South? Go north to Washington D.C.? Thankfully, God had an incredible plan for me. A few months before graduation, I learned about an opportunity to teach overseas with my friend and sorority sister Leigh. *Perfect. I can postpone the real world just a little longer by living in one of the most beautiful and romantic cities in the world—Prague!* Great for the risk taker; not so great for the single (read: lonely) gal.

To my surprise, when I first arrived in Prague, I experienced a huge sense of isolation and vulnerability. I had experienced these emotions before, but never to such a degree. While my friendship with Leigh and others I met were temporary remedies for my lonesome soul, life in a foreign country (where you barely speak the language or understand the culture) proved to be difficult. Instead of praying for things like a husband, health and a husband, and so on, I prayed for electricity, emotional peace and safety. Sure, I had money in my checking account, warm clothes and a passport, but this new life required a level of dependence on God that I had never encountered before.

Growing up in a God-centered home, I had perfected the Christian good-girl image. I read my Bible, went to church, memorized Scripture; in essence, I did what I thought every good Christian should do. But I was missing the point. I was not *experiencing* God. My time in Prague, where I was stripped raw of my comforts and sense of security, allowed me to experience God in a way I did not imagine possible. My awe of Him increased tremendously as I felt Him always, talked to Him daily and grew deeply in love with my Savior. I soon discovered that I can survive with very few "things," but I am doomed without God and the adventure, community and relationship—romantic or otherwise—that He offers me. Even with these struggles (or maybe because of them), my Prague days were some of my very best. I was independent, challenged and doing something I really loved.

When I committed to my overseas adventure, I had planned from the start to eventually return to the States. Two years went quickly, and as the end of my time in Prague drew near, I realized that my soul desperately needed some R & R. As much as I knew that God was calling me to move back home (literally, back down the hall from Mom and Dad), I worried that my spirit would dry up in suburbia. I feared that what I had gained in Prague—a love of travel and teaching—was only for a season, or worse, reserved for a time in my life when I was without common distractions like gorgeous American men who smelled wonderful and had clearly been to the dentist in the last, oh, five years.

In July 2003, I packed up and said good-bye to my "glamorous" big-city European life.

Since returning to California, I've watched siblings, friends, coworkers and roommates fall in love and get married. Once referred to as "roomie," "best friend," or "bridesmaid," I am now "Aunt Megs" to the babies of those same siblings, friends, coworkers and former roommates. As I look at how different my life is compared to theirs, I can't help but wonder if I've missed the relationship boat altogether? *I* want to be The Fiancée, The Bride, The Mom.

Not one to just let life happen, but participate in everything, I decided to take action. Good-bye, single girl. Hello, The World's Best Dating Service.

2

Let the Games Begin

When I decided to join The World's Best Dating Service, I was not a dating service virgin. I had tried at least three online dating services—at one point trying to balance two of them at the same time. Casting a wide net seemed to be the best approach. Unfortunately, my plan was not foolproof. Before long, I had what felt like a part-time job looking at three-by-three-inch online photos that had most likely been photo-shopped to remove inches, add hair and whiten whatever needed whitening. After two months, I had too many online pen pals to count, one face-to-face date and an unchanged relationship status on my Facebook page. Sure, I subjected myself to these online methods, hoping to meet a great man with whom I could start a relationship. However, I did not think it was too much to ask for a few dates out of the deal.

Eventually, when those online subscriptions expired (or when I canceled them due to my impatience), a serious case of "What do I have to lose?" syndrome kicked in. Symptoms usually include worry, indecision, regret and a heightened sense of curiosity about what I might be missing. I was so focused on what I did not have (a boyfriend) that I failed to see what I did have: girlfriends with boyfriends, coworkers who were blissful newlyweds, brothers who had married up, parents who were still deeply in love and dinner invites where I was the only single person in the room. Of course, God had been good to me, but it can be hard to see the blessings beyond the Friday nights alone.

So I refocused. And I prayed. I asked others to pray for me. I asked God to show me what *He* desires for me, not what I want for myself. The prayer went something like this: "Thank You for my singleness. Since I am single and not dating a man who loves You and happens to look like _____ (in my case, Christian Bale), I can only assume that YOU, my Savior, are all I need right now and You will provide more when the time is right." While I know that was the "right" thing to pray, it was still really hard for me to let go of the fact that I felt like God was ignoring my heart's desire.

A few months after celebrating my birthday in Chicago with me, Leigh and Amanda arrived in late August for an end-of-summer last hurrah. Amanda was our third *amiga* in Prague, and we try to get together once a year. We pass the days lounging by the pool, walking the beach, deep in conversation and drowning in laughter. Since dating never really goes off my radar and seems to be the destination of many of my conversations, we spend some time talking about our love lives. We're all single and doing our best to encourage each other to trust God, stay positive and be patient. Of course, I am not taking any of my own advice about patience as I immediately bring up my new idea of trying another dating service (the same one I had mentioned to my dad). The girls think it's a great idea, and by the end of the week, I have made an appointment with The World's Best Dating Service, and Leigh has signed up for a free trial with an online service. It will be a race to the altar. Amanda will cheer from the sidelines . . . at least for now.

* * *

The elevator doors open and I am face to face with a nicely dressed man accompanied by his college-aged daughter. I step in and assume the official elevator position. As the three of us watch the numbers above the doors descend, the man says, "Dating service, huh?"

What?! Oh, my gosh . . . is it obvious? Can everyone tell just by looking at me that moments ago I joined a dating service?

Heart speeding up.

Is it hot in here?

Sweating.

Are the walls really closing in?

Breathe, Megan, breathe.

The dapper man continues, "Since my office is right next to theirs, I frequently see people who have just interviewed with the service. I think it's a great idea. I'm trying to convince my daughter here to try it." My heart rate returns to normal. The daughter looks at me with eyes that say, "I will never be desperate enough to try a dating service. Are you kidding me, Dad?"

Doors open. "Well, good luck," he says.

And thus begins my experience with The World's Best Dating Service.

When I first set foot in their offices, I am greeted by a friendly receptionist who ushers me into a small room. Apparently there has been a special on primary colored furniture at IKEA, and the office decorator has purchased one of everything. This waiting room makes me feel like I am at daycare. The receptionist hands me a clipboard with a thick stack of paperwork attached. Not unlike the doctor's office or DMV, this paperwork is tedious and repetitive. "Profession" (*History teacher*). "Please explain your profession" (*Eight hours a day spent enlightening today's youth on topics such as Chinese dynasties, world religions and geographic features*). Unlike the doctor's office or DMV, questions included "Describe your last boyfriend in 50 words or less" (*Distant, with potential commitment issues*) and "What does romance mean to you?" (*A lot; I'm female*) and "On a scale of 1 to 10, how important is physical appearance?" (*A five+ if they are over six feet tall . . . a seven if they are under five foot eleven*). Buried in a list of countless boxes where you check things that apply to you, and in between "morning person" and "enjoys reading" was "Christian." I checked the box. I figured I'd have an opportunity to explain later how much weight that little checkmark carried.

Just as I was finishing up the questions, Jessica entered and introduced herself as head matchmaker. She began to thumb through my paperwork. "So, what happened with your last boyfriend?" *Wow, no icebreaker questions or warm up?*

"Unfortunately, it was a long-distance relationship, and seeing as he was my first boyfriend, I felt very unsure of myself and my dating skills. Great guy, a lot of fun, but in the end, he wanted me to be something I was not. I came to the relationship with very little baggage and I think that made him uncomfortable. I guess he prefers women who over pack." I crack a joke to cover my nerves. Jessica does not laugh.

Moving right along, she says, "Okay, I get that. Now tell me, what are some of the things that are 'musts' for you in a relationship?"

Here goes . . . "The most important thing for me is someone who shares the same faith I have. It's my ultimate non-negotiable. I am a Christian, and that is a very large part of my life. I know that means different things to people, but to me, it means that my belief in God is my compass. My relationship with Him directs my decisions and my actions and is the foundation of any romantic relationship."

"That makes sense," she says.

I continue to explain. "I am not expecting a man to bring his Bible to our date, or necessarily bring it up at our first meeting, but I do want someone who goes to church and would be willing to go with me. I can't be with someone who is not interested in this part of my life and ultimately doesn't want to share in that with me."

I stop talking, feeling confident that I have expressed myself well.

"Great," she says. "Now, name five celebrities that you find attractive."

Really, Jessica? That's it? You don't need me to explain that whole Christian thing? Are you sure you got that? (George Clooney, the aforementioned Christian Bale, Patrick Dempsey, Anderson Cooper, John Krasinski.) I go on to talk about a desire for kids, the need for a tall man, a low handicap on the golf course, a love of traveling, dependability, someone I can respect and, of course, a man who would be confident enough to sit on the same side of the booth at a restaurant (*Yeah, I know . . . most people think that's lame. Embrace it, you know you want to try it.*)

While most of the interview was basic formality, I did feel that Jessica took an interest in me and my search for "The One." Maybe she moonlights as an actress, but I left the office feeling as though she really wanted me to meet someone, and that she was sincere in her promise that there were plenty of Christian men (some of whom she was already thinking) who would be good matches for me. I think in the sales world this is what they call "closing the deal." It worked.

After a one-and-a-half-hour interview, I had been told that I'm a "catch" (*"Never heard that one before," says the author as she rolls her eyes*), any man would love to date me and of course they have a plethora of potentials they can set me up with. Jessica snaps a quick Polaroid of me and says she'll be right back.

Wait, let me take a look at the Polaroid! Were my eyes closed? Do I have something in my teeth? I know none of my dates will see the photo, but all the women in the office will, and women can be so cruel and catty. I fear the picture is worse than what is on my driver's license.

Jessica returns with contract in hand. "You're guaranteed 14 dates, but I'm sure you'll have more than that. I have such confidence that this will work for you. You can't look at any of the men's pictures or files, but we will call you within the next week to give you your first match. And don't worry, after we describe him to you, you can say no if you don't like what we're offering. After each date you will call us with feedback, and by date five or six, we should have the perfect match for you."

Sign contract.

Open purse.

Pull out wallet.

Hand over MasterCard.

At least I am getting airline miles even if I don't get a husband out of the deal.

Gentlemen, on your mark . . . there's a new girl in the dating pool . . . hope you can catch her.

3

Humanistic Henry

. . . .

"You have one new message. Message sent Tuesday at 3:30."

An overly peppy voice that resembles a cheerleader on Red Bull says, "Hi, Megan! This is Bridget from The World's Best Dating Service. I wanted to tell you about a great match I have for you. His name is Henry, and I think you'd be awesome together. Call me back and we'll set something up."

"Henry"... interesting. Nothing wrong with that name, but I must say, I don't know anyone named Henry under the age of, well ... 70.

So here it begins, four days after signing my dating life away, we have our first contestant.

I call Bridget back. Though it's only three rings, it seems an eternity before she picks up. "Hi, Bridget, it's Megan. Thanks for calling." My voice is friendly but not matching her pep in any way.

"Megan, I am so glad you called back. Let me tell you about Henry. He's six feet tall, dark brown hair, 24 (*What?! I did not pay to rob the cradle*), an investment banker who played college baseball and loves golf (*Scratch that, younger is okay*). And to top it all off, he is writing a book (*Hopefully, not about his experience with the dating service*)!"

"Okay, sounds like a good start," I say. "When and where can I meet him, Bridget?" I'm in; feet first, ready to go. Am I really that eager to go on a date? Apparently so. It's been a long time.

Over the next day or two, through a series of voicemails, Bridget is able to set up a time and place for us to meet. My stomach's been in knots since the first call when Bridget told me about Henry. When you lack serious dating skills, you can't help but get painfully nervous before, during and sometimes even after a date. I've got some qualified experience with nerves; nerves were the whole reason I retired from my basketball career at the ripe old age of 17. I would literally throw up before each game. Thankfully, I have not reached that point with dating . . . yet.

Fast forward to Sunday night. I filled the day with people and activities in an attempt to keep my mind occupied—church in the morning, a midday game of tennis and a short nap. At 5:30, I drive to The Cheesecake Factory and "pep talk" myself all the way. *Megan, you can do this. It's one date; the first five minutes will be the worst, but you'll survive. You're in a public place; it's safe.* I enter the restaurant walking tall, publicly confident and inwardly meek; I tell the waiflike hostess—who doesn't look more than 14—that I have a seven o'clock reservation under the name of Megan or Henry. Since the dating service sets up everything in advance, the reservation is placed under both names.

"Oh, you're with that dating service, how fun!" she says, all too cheerfully and louder than I'd hoped for. *Inside voice, please, my dear.* The restaurant goes silent. Diners from every direction turn and look at me. "Dating service! Yikes!" they all seem to say. Apparently The World's Best Dating Service does not coach the hostess on how *not* to make their clients feel like losers. Perhaps I'm too sensitive; if I heard the hostess at a restaurant say these words, you bet I'd strain my neck to see who it was that needs a dating service to meet people.

"Henry is right over there." She raises her arm and with a smile points me toward a young man in the corner of the lobby, bachelor #1. I see Henry and think "cute." His dark hair is wavy and cut short. His eyes are dark and friendly; his smile kind with just a touch of confidence, or is that arrogance? A bit like Andy Garcia. More Andy than Garcia. He's wearing the male version of the Orange County dating uniform: jeans and a long-sleeved button-down shirt, untucked of course. I scan down to the shoes, expecting to see black loafer-esque slip-ons. Instead I see he's wearing a pair of size 12, blinding white Adidas tennis shoes. *Eew! Bad choice, Henry.* (I promise I am not a snob; I just appreciate a man with a good fashion sense.) No worries . . . if we start dating, I can fix that. Always the optimist.

The tactless hostess takes us to our table. We're seated and I instantly start talking more than necessary. "How are you?" (which I am sure I said more than once). "Have you been here before?" *He's here with you, Megan, no need to try and reel him in with a lame pick-up line! Pace yourself.*

Food's ordered and we finally get past the pleasantries of a first date. Before long, here is what I know about Henry: He is originally from the Bay area, has a twin (*maybe the twin has the Garcia of Andy Garcia*), went to a Catholic university here in Southern California, was a catcher on the baseball team and has a close relationship with his family, especially with his Grandmother. At this point I feel safe with Henry and have finally calmed down enough to actually enjoy myself. There were a few uncomfortable moments, but that is to be expected. It's rare that a first date is not awkward in some way or another. During a conversation lull, I ask Henry about the book he is writing.

He smiles with pride and starts in, "It's a how-to guide for 20-somethings interested in buying real estate as investments. I'm writing the book from the perspective of my grandmother and all the advice she's given me over the years."

"Interesting. I like the idea of writing it from her perspective. Do you have a favorite piece of advice that she's offered?" I truly am curious.

"She's a crazy old bird." *Henry, I know that most people have one or two crazy relatives somewhere in their family (not in mine, of course), but do you really want to advertise that? At this point I am wondering how far this apple has fallen from that tree. Maybe it skips a generation? But then our kids would be doomed. Please, Megan, why are you wasting your time thinking about this?*

He continues, "My favorite is the time she took a greyhound bus from her retirement home in Tampa all the way to Atlantic City and came home 20K richer. When she got home, instead of spending that money on a trip or a new car, she invested all her winnings in a new doublewide. She may be crazy, but she is smart!" His enthusiasm strikes me as a bit over the top.

While I realize this is only one antidote from Henry's book, I am a bit skeptical. Let me get this straight: in order to have money to invest in real estate, I need to gamble. Huh, not a bad plan, but a bit risky. I don't think many 20-somethings need encouragement to gamble; weekends in Vegas happen pretty naturally. And while I'm not an expert, I am pretty confident that most people come home from those weekends poorer, not richer, and generally hung over.

Over the course of the next hour we finish our meal and continue to chat. We cover family histories, travels and favorite pets. All in all, the conversation's relaxed and fun. At the end of the night we walk out into the parking garage and before parting ways exchange numbers. Henry shakes my hand, which is fine with me; it is a first date after all. He calls me a few days later and we set up date number two.

Henry and I both had Thursday afternoon free, and a casual coffee date seemed like a good choice for date number two. Summer was drawing to a close and I had been at work all day, setting up my classroom. I was less nervous for the second round, knowing that we had plenty in common and should have no problem finding things to talk about. I was anticipating relaxing a bit with a chai tea and Henry. What I did not anticipate was the speed in which this date would begin to go downhill. Turns out, Henry is a humanist. He didn't call himself that, but in my opinion, it fits. As we're waiting for the barista to whip up our drinks, Henry asked me what I was doing over the weekend, specifically on Sunday night. I could not tell if he was asking because he had already decided he wanted to see me again or if he figured it was a safe place to start our conversation. I told him I go to church on Sunday nights with friends and then out to dinner afterwards.

He paused for a second and then said, "Do you go to church every weekend?"

"Not every weekend, but most," I say.

"So it's a big part of your life."

"Yes. It's really important to me." I hesitate to say more because I don't want to make him uncomfortable, but naturally, I follow up that statement with, "What about you? Do you attend church?" Seems nonthreatening enough.

"Well, I did go to Catholic school, so I went to mass a lot. Now I go on Christmas Eve and Easter just to make my parents happy." Henry goes on to tell me he believes we all have some kind of divine power inside of us. We are the "masters of our own destiny" and don't really need the church. Unfortunately, that does not jive with my Presbyterian upbringing. I change the subject and while the rest of our date is pleasant, it was no shock that Henry never called me again. Maybe he did not like Presbyterians.

The World's Best Dating Service asks that I call them within 24 hours with feedback on my date. It's their way of getting me closer and closer to "The One."

Following the rules, I leave a voicemail the very next day: "Hi, Bridget, it's Megan Carson. Henry was nice, and it was a great first date for me (*once I got past the shoes, of course*). We had a similar sense of humor and similar interests, but we don't seem to be compatible in the area of religion. Remember, that is a big part of my life. I'm looking forward to meeting someone else, so bring it on." Click. *Oh, Lord. Did I really say, "Bring it on"? Now I sound like the cheerleader.*

Postscript

More than a year after my date with Henry, we meet again. Well, kind of. Oddly, I spot him at the Christmas Eve service I was attending with my family. *Henry, you are a man of your word! You told me you attended church on Christmas Eve and Easter and here you are.* Wait . . . maybe he goes to church more often? There is no way for me to know this or not, but it's quite possible that he now attends church on a regular basis. I laugh and think, *Of course he goes to church now, and not when I met him.* Regardless of the circumstances or how frequently he attends, I am glad he's here.

As if ordained by God, I am seated where I can see him but he can't see me. When the service is over, I am quick to duck behind my six-foot-four dad to ensure that Henry doesn't see me, but I most definitely keep a clear view of him . . . and the cute young lady that he's holding hands with. Ahh, he's found someone, and they appear to be quite into each other. It seems The World's Best Dating Service was a success for him! As they leave the sanctuary, I see just how perfect they are together. He's wearing those same white tennis shoes and she's wearing platform flip-flops with her wool skirt and cardigan. A match made in shoe heaven. *See you at Easter, Henry!*

· ·

4

Billionaire Bachelor

It's a Monday night, about three weeks since my date with Henry, and I am back at The Cheesecake Factory ready for match number two. I pray there is a different hostess on duty—one that won't blow my cover. Bridget has informed me that tonight's match is an all-American type of guy who lives in Newport Beach. He's originally from Connecticut and played football at a university in the Northeast. He loves golf and is a chemist. What? An all-American chemist? Sounds like an oxymoron. Oh well . . . he could be The One, right? Let's just hope he has decent shoes.

This particular Monday night happens to be the first Monday Night Football game of the season. As a huge sports fan, I was a bit conflicted about accepting a date on this night. Wouldn't I rather be on my favorite blue couch snuggled up to a bowl of chips and salsa, getting ready for some football? Well, yes. However I asked myself why I would pass up a potentially great date just to watch football. A better plan would be to go on the date and possibly have something other than a bowl of chips beside me on the couch at next week's game.

As I restlessly wait near the hostess stand, I check out every blond guy who walks through the door. Here comes a blond . . . hope it's not him . . . too short. And another . . . oops . . . awkward moment of eye contact before I quickly turn away. Then a third . . . ooh, I hope it's him! Thankfully, this blond heads straight for me. Bingo! Jackpot! J.Crew prepster with shaggy blond hair meets Orange County laid-back cool. Perfectly crisp blue oxford shirt tucked into a hip pair of jeans. Brown belt matches brown deck shoes. Stellar first impression, Jason.

Our eyes meet. "Are you Megan?"

"Yes. Are you Jason?" I'm sure I'm blushing.

"Yes, good to meet you," he says, extending a hand for me to shake.

I accept his firm and friendly handshake. "Likewise." (*Likewise? I never say likewise!*) "How did you know it was me?" I ask, slightly out of breath, my heart bouncing around in my throat.

"Well, the dating service told me you were a pretty brunette with blue eyes and about five foot nine. You were the first person I saw who fit that description." Now I'm definitely blushing. First down for Jason. I must admit, I love a man with confidence. He had no qualms about walking right up to me. Worst-case scenario, it was not me and he moves on to the other (albeit less attractive) brunettes in the restaurant.

Over drinks and the breadbasket we get to know each other a bit. Like most first dates, I'm trying to make it not feel like a job interview or a stand-up comedy routine. I attempt to tease my date with enough of my good traits so he'll be anxious for more. Thirty minutes into our date, I'm fully convinced that Jason has a lot going for him. He's well-educated, widely traveled, funny, attractive and a great conversationalist. *I'm so glad I signed up for this service,* I say to myself. He's also genuinely friendly and slightly flirty. However, he flirts like a girl. His shaggy golden hair falls into his eyes and every few minutes he casually tosses his head to the right, resulting in the equivalent of a female hair flip, a girl's ace-in-the-hole flirt tactic. Funny thing is, I totally dig it.

I've been told guys love it when girls can talk about sports, and knowing Jason played college football, I pull my "go-to" card and bring up my love of sports. I tell Jason I'm shocked that he agreed to a date on the season opener of Monday Night Football. "Oh, a football fan?" he says with a smile. First down for Megan! Jason playfully suggests we move our date into the bar where we can watch the game . . . and we do.

Once in the bar, Jason shares that he's a member at an exclusive Country Club in Newport Beach. Now, to many people this would translate into some serious bragging, but I'm impressed. More importantly, my dad will be impressed. My dad has raised a woman who knows the best golf courses in the area. (This is a dad who wants me to marry a professional golfer so when he retires he can follow his son-in-law around on the PGA tour.) Membership at Jason's course is not cheap; just ask Tiger Woods and Mark McGuire. At this point, I happen to know that, and instantly Jason is no longer "Jason," but in my mind he's officially "Billionaire Bachelor." Okay, "billionaire" might be a stretch, but a girl can dream.

Over cheeseburgers and the din of the football game I learn that Jason was previously engaged to a woman whose father was a Baptist minister, spends every Sunday night having dinner with his parents and loves to grill. I'm sure Jason learned something about me as well, but I was not thinking about me, I was single-mindedly focused on my very own Owen Wilson.

The plates are cleared, the game ends and to my pleasant surprise Jason pays the bill. (The World's Best Dating Service recommends that you go Dutch, but Jason said that's not his style. *Perfect, it's not mine either*.) Outside the restaurant, Jason asks for my number, gives me a hug and we part ways. I walk to my car, oblivious to the world around me. I am postdate delirious.

On the way home, I call my dad, but it goes straight to voicemail. "Dad. It's too bad you're married, because I have found the perfect match for you. Jason is a responsible and successful chemist, loves sports and has a six handicap. Not to mention he's a member at that exclusive club in Newport. He did ask for my number . . . stay tuned."

By Wednesday of that week, we have date number two set— dinner and a movie on Sunday night. Wednesday night, I remember that I need to call the dating service with my feedback. So much for following their orders. "Bridget, Jason was a really good match for me. We hit it off and had plenty in common. We're going out again on Sunday. I am looking forward to learning more about him. Well done!"

* * * *

Even though it's only Friday, the nerves have kicked in. THIS is what I hate about dating. Sitting around waiting for the date to arrive, thinking about all the possible scenarios. Could this be my last "second date" ever? Will we have anything else to talk about? What am I going to wear? What will I say when I see him? This unrelenting battery of questions that haunt me at the start of any possible relationship is why I am researching convents in Italy. If I am going to be a nun (*Wait, is there an equivalent for a Protestant?*), then I'm going to at least be a nun in a beautiful place. But there are so many good-looking men in Italy—that could be a potential problem. Okay, I'll become a nun in Siberia. Then there will be no distractions. I can focus only on my service to the Lord.

Late Friday night, while watching a movie with some friends, I get a text message from Jason. Since text has become the communication mode of choice for my generation, I don't think much of it. (Now, if he is only texting and never picking up the phone, we'll have to have a conversation about that.) The text explains that The Country Club is having a luau party on Saturday. Would I like to go to that instead of the movie on Sunday? Jason also asks if I'd like to bring a friend to make it more comfortable, and he would provide a date for her as well. *How nice. He knows that a party at this country club might be a bit intimidating, so he's going to let me bring a friend.* Before I know it, I've sent Jason a text and committed myself, and my sweet roommate Allison, to a night of leis, limbo and libations at the luau. *Safety in numbers,* I tell myself. Jason promises to call me in the morning with all the details.

Around one o'clock on Saturday, I get a phone call from Jason. He tells me he's been at the golf course all morning. A guy in his foursome hit a hole-in-one, and they have been celebrating at the bar since eleven. "I've already had too much to drink. Actually, I'm pretty dunk." Loud laughter ensues. *Already too much to drink, at one o'clock? TMI (Too Much Information), Jason, TMI.* He also tells me that he can't find a date for Allison, and the youngest person on the guest list for the luau is about 50.

"Can we just go back to our original plan of dinner and a movie tomorrow night?" He asks a bit timidly, as if I'm going to be raging mad because of the change in plans.

"Sure. Can I still bring Allison?" I joke. Silence on the other end.

"Um . . . well . . ."

"I was just kidding; I promise not to bring a chaperone." Again, not laughing.

Tough crowd. So it's back to Plan A.

Sunday morning, I wake up and head to church with Allison and our friend Amy. After the service we stop for pancakes at The Original Pancake House. Over pancakes, bacon and coffee Amy asks if I'm nervous about my date. "Um, yes! Did you not notice I ordered one pancake when I normally get a full stack?" I ask sarcastically

"Appetite's gone, not sleeping well, nervous fidgeting . . ." Allison tallies my symptoms. "Classic signs of date-induced anxiety!"

We laugh.

"I'm not very confident in my dating skills; I hope we'll have enough to talk about. I am a really self-conscious dater," I admit. Being the true friends they are, Allison and Amy build me up with encouragement. They say all the right things: just be yourself, it will be fun, he's nervous too! I leave the restaurant encouraged and excited about meeting up that night with Jason.

Back home, I'm just laying down for a nice afternoon nap (yes, I am not ashamed that I love naps) when my phone rings. It's Jason.

"Hello," I answer cheerfully with a small hint of a question mark.

"Hi, Megan, it's Jason. I am going to have to cancel our date for tonight. Some of my clients are visiting from Australia, and since they leave tomorrow morning, I need to take them out for dinner tonight. I am sorry to cancel last minute like this."

"No worries, Jason. I know things come up." Ever the agreeable one, I let him off the hook.

"I'll call you tomorrow to reschedule. I do want to see you again."

"Great. I'd like that. Hope tonight goes well. Talk to you soon." Disappointed, yet slightly relieved, I suddenly realize I'm starving. Without a moment to lose, I jump out of bed and head for the fridge.

Sadly, my Billionaire Bachelor earned a new nickname in the following days: Billionaire Bust. Yep, I never heard from him again. Sure, I thought of all the scenarios. It's possible he got into a gnarly car accident, and because he had not told anyone about me yet, no one knew to call me. It's imaginable that he lost my number, and since the dating service is not allowed to give out personal info, he was never able to get my number back. It's conceivable that he met another girl and within 24 hours they ran to Vegas and got married by Elvis.

Or maybe, just maybe, there's a teeny-tiny possibility that he wasn't interested.

I called my dad to tell him the devastating news. "Dad, it's Megan. I'm sorry, but I don't think you'll be teeing it up with Jason, my Billionaire Bachelor, anytime soon. I did my best, but he and I were not a match. Basically, he never called me back for a second date. Yeah, truth hurts, but . . . oh well."

Two down, 12 to go.

. . . .

5

F-Bomb Bill

. . . .

Two-and-a-half weeks into football season (and now over Billionaire Bust), I was anxious to meet my next match. The World's
Best Dating Service proposed a lunch date for bachelor number
three. I liked the idea of having a limited amount of time with
my mystery date; if it was a mess from the start, we both had an
out. I know, I know, I should stay positive. My schedule rarely
permits me to leave work during the lunch hour (in my case the
lunch half-hour), but my school had a minimum day schedule,
so I agreed to meet Bill over lunch. Yes, most people are very jeal-
ous of teachers and their 7:00 to 3:00 workday. What they don't
realize is that within those eight hours, teachers rarely get a
chance to sit down or use the restroom and are under the constant threat of mutiny as they're outnumbered 35 to 1. For a
teacher, going "out to lunch" is an unheard of delight!

I meet Bill at a typical Mexican place with far too many terra-
cotta colors going on, fake plants, vinyl booths (that stick like
glue to exposed flesh) and tables topped in brightly colored tiles.
While I don't love this place, the free chips and salsa can be
counted on to raise my spirits. I'm also pretty excited to be escap-
ing school during the lunch hour. And, oh, that's right, I'm here
on a date! I should be excited about meeting Bill too. But I'm
not. Nothing against Bill, but since I was burned by Billionaire
Bachelor, I'm feeling a bit wounded. Had I been a frequent dater,

and not a serial single gal, I think I would recover more quickly
from dates that didn't work. Instead I waste a lot of energy ana-
lyzing the situation over and over until I realize the simple fact
is that he has moved on and I had better do the same.

As I walk into the restaurant, I see my five-foot-nine blond
sitting in the waiting area playing with his cell phone. His leg is
bouncing up and down and he is working the phone like a text
message champ. *I'm sorry, Bill, but the moment I saw you I wanted to
turn around and grab the valet guy (who was rather cute, by the way)
before he parked my car.* I just had this feeling. Most call it a gut
feeling, but I know it was the Holy Spirit. I had a sense that this
was not going to be a good date. I kind of wish the Holy Spirit
had pulled an Old Testament maneuver and struck me down,
because what transpired next was a first for me and I wish I
could have avoided it. I froze in fear and considered leaving. Of
course I would never actually do it, but what's the harm in considering a quick exit?

Instead of jumping ship, I make my way to the bathroom
just to delay the inevitable. After stalling for a good five minutes, I look myself in the mirror and give the pep talk: "Come
on, Megan. You can do this. It's only lunch!"

Bypassing the hostess, I walk up to Bill and introduce myself.
He shoves the phone into his pocket; we exchange an awkward
hello and follow the hostess to the table. I wonder if I'm not what
he is expecting, because he is certainly not what I was expecting. I
am wearing two-inch heels and am taller than him. Apparently,
five foot nine really means five foot seven on a good day. Women
lie about their weight. Men lie about their height. I start thinking
about Sonny and Cher, Tom and Nicole, Tom and Katie, Nicole
and Keith. The I'm-taller-than-my-man-and-proud-of-it look is
in right now. *Maybe I should reconsider this height thing.*

The hostess takes us to a horseshoe-shaped booth and it's
clear that neither of us really knows where to sit. These booths

work wonders for five or six people but are demeaning to a party of two who've only met three minutes prior in the lobby. You either sit uncomfortably close or miles apart. In the end, we clumsily settle on the opposite edges of the horseshoe, as distant from each other as possible. Okay, here goes.

Bill clears his throat to break the silence and starts in. "So, I hear you're a teacher. What grade?"

"Ninth and tenth."

"Dang, girl. What's that like?"

"Dang, girl"? I'll just pretend that he never said that. For some reason people are usually surprised to learn that I am a high school teacher. Maybe I look too young. Maybe they hated high school and would never consider spending more time there. Regardless of Bill's reasons, I proceed into my standard response. "I really love teaching. It's a perfect fit for me." I say things like "it's my passion," "teens are so entertaining," "I'm often mistaken for a student, being so young, and cute and all." I finish with "What's funny is that I actually teach at the high school I graduated from."

"You gotta be effen kidding me . . . you teach at the same school you graduated from?"

"You gotta be effen kidding me?!"

Four minutes and 39 seconds into the date and an F-Bomb has been dropped.

Oh, no, he didn't! Check, please!

Now, I know that people cuss. And, believe it or not, I, too, have said a bad word in my lifetime. But come on. Really, Bill? You're going to pull this on a first date? Either you are trying to impress me (*Not working, Bill. Not . . . working.*) or you cuss so frequently that you have no clue you just dropped an F-Bomb. You guessed it, the latter.

Bill continues to talk, and I find comfort drowning myself in the endless chips and salsa. I discover he sells paper (that's where the similarities to Jim Halpert end), is originally from a state that has a Great Lake named after it, loves to wake board and spends at least two weekends a month in Vegas. F-Bomb count: six.

Side note: Here is something you should know about me. I am constantly working on improving that little skill called confrontation. I am confident, considerate, consistent, sometimes confused; but I'm just not good at confronting. Getting better, but there is plenty of room to grow. Looking back, I had every right to confront Bill and say something like: "Bill, I know that I hardly know you, but something you should know about me is that I don't appreciate the frequency of your use of the F-Bomb. While I understand that you might be trying to use the word to add emphasis to a stirring comment, or show anger, I firmly believe a date—a first date no less—is not the time or place for such language. I would appreciate it if you would refrain from cussing in my presence for the remainder of our time together." Of course this would have been quite patronizing and have made no sense to Bill. If I was going to tell him to put a kibosh on the cussing, it needed to be in language he could relate to. Something more like: "Bill, what in the hell are you doing? Give it a rest with the F-Bomb, already. I don't appreciate it!"

I said nothing, and the cussing continued.

I'm almost done with my taquitos (the chips and salsa were sucked dry) when Bill drops another kind of bomb.

"By the way, today is my birthday!"

Oh jeez, what do I say to that? Well, obviously "Happy Birthday," or in this case, "Happy effen Birthday!" Should I feel sorry for Bill? He is spending his birthday lunch with a total stranger on a blind date. Do I excuse myself to use the restroom only to tell our waiter that it's Bill's birthday and could he round up as many people as possible to sing to him? Do you have a mariachi band? A huge sombrero we could put on his head? Anything to embarrass the heck out of him? Didn't Bill have some friends who wanted to take him out on his big day? I hope he does not expect me to pay for his meal. Should I pay for it? This is absolutely a first for me. I am beginning to miss my 30-minute lunch chocked down in the teacher's lounge.

Rounding up the Birthday Brigade would be too much effort, and thankfully our conversation has come to a standstill. I tell Bill that I need to head back to school to get some papers graded. (Really, I just want to bolt across the street to South Coast Plaza and the half-yearly sale at Nordstrom.) The waitress has already brought the check, so we both pull out our wallets. I think for a moment about paying for his lunch, but the thought passes, and we go Dutch.

"I really enjoyed meeting you, Megan. I am going to Las Vegas this weekend (*SHOCKER!*), but maybe we could get together next week. Can I give you a call?" In one of my weaker moments, I actually hand Bill my number.

Sure, Bill, give me a call. I won't answer the effen call or call you back . . . but whatever!

We head to the door and all of a sudden Bill says, "Eff! I left my valet ticket on the table. I'm going to go back and get it. See ya."

I proceed to the valet station and hand over my ticket. You would have thought I was a woman running from the law—fidgeting with my purse and looking over my shoulder as I wait for my Honda. Unbelievably, my car arrives in record time. As I drive off, I see Bill standing at the valet. He waves and I give him the birdie.

No, I didn't really give him the birdie. I am not that bold or quick on my feet. And, well, it's just not nice; with my luck, someone I know would have seen it. Inevitably they would tell my parents and then my mom would call and inform me that ladies don't behave in such a way and I need to call Bill immediately and tell him I am very sorry. But if there was ever a time that I should have been rebellious . . .

6

Besos Ben = Besos Breakdown

. . . .

The very next day, Monica (one of the many of dating service matchmakers) calls to tell me about my next match. Whoa . . . slow down. I need some serious time to recover from that disaster of a date less than 24 hours ago. Before Monica can say anything else, I give her an earful about Bill.

"Oh, my, that date bombed!" she says.

"Literally," I reply.

"Well, don't worry, this next match is top-notch."

Ben is his name. He's five foot nine (pictures of Tom and Katie Cruise return to my mind) and from the Midwest. He looks just like a well-known celebrity and loves being outdoors. And, he's a Christian. Do I want to meet him? What time and where? Monica says she will call me tomorrow with all the details of the date.

Though Ben sounds great, I begin to think The World's Best Dating Service has a lot of vertically challenged men joining their service. They have yet to provide me with a match over six feet tall. Now, no offense to my "less-tall" male friends, but when you're a female who is five foot nine, with brothers and a father who are all over six foot two, you tend to prefer taller men.

After I hang up the phone I head straight for my closet to pull out every pair of flats I own. Staring at five lonely shoes (yes, one was a single . . . of course!) I realize that every shoe looked like it came from my grandma's closet. I remembered my aunt telling me about the time she bought five pairs of flats on one shopping trip because she'd fallen in love with a shorter man. She knew she'd never wear heels again. Though I'd yet to fall in love, Ben made the perfect excuse for a trip to Nordstrom's shoe department. Nothing but the best for my future with a shorter-than-me man. Since flats are currently a fashion "yes," I had no problem finding a pair that looked like they belonged in *my* closet. Walking to my car, silver shopping bag in hand, I think, *Too bad The World's Best Dating Service doesn't have such good selection.*

Two nights later, wearing my new golden flats, I set off to meet Ben at Bellissimo. This popular Italian café is definitely a step up from The Cheesecake Factory or less-than-stellar Mexican food. I valet my car and nervously enter the restaurant where Hugh Jackman greets me. No—actually it's Ben, but he's a dead ringer for the adorable Aussie. Well-dressed and wearing a big smile, he stands up to greet me. Yep, I'm definitely taller. Feeling like my gold flats have failed me, I remind myself to keep an open mind. *Megan. It's not his fault he's short!*

We're led to an L-shaped booth and have no problem sliding into comfortable spots to sit. We sit fairly close, but don't worry, we were not "same-side boothing." Conversation ensues and there's an instant connection on my end. My heart begins to race; I'm equal parts nervous and calm; I want to make a good impression. I try not to fidget. Right leg is bouncing. My eye starts to twitch. *Quick, say something!*

"Have you been here before, Ben?" *Good save.*

"No, I have not." *Why on earth did I ask a yes or no question?*

A moment of silence, then Ben breaks it. "I know the dating service suggests we go Dutch, but please order whatever you want. Dinner is on me. My mother would never forgive me for letting a woman pay."

Your mom sounds like a wonderful woman.

"That's sweet of you, Ben. Thanks!"

When the waiter approaches, asking if we'd like an appetizer, without hesitation Ben orders us a shrimp cocktail and a bottle of wine. I have no problem with the wine but realize that I am going to have to gag down the shrimp. Sorry, Ben, I don't like shrimps. I don't mean you, being a little short and all; I mean actual shrimp.

Our appetizer is delivered, and thankfully we're talking so much that I don't think Ben realized I only ate one shrimp. I begin to relax and enjoy myself, Ben laughs at my jokes, and only once do I put my foot in my mouth—I ask him what college he graduated from. He tells me he did not finish college. *No big deal. I know school is not for everyone. I'll just wait until we're dating seriously to tell my dad you're not a college grad.*

Our pasta arrives and I learn more about Ben's family. His brother is a pastor and his sister works for a Christian ministry. (Insert small sense of hope in my heart.) I don't want to assume too much, but this is a step in the right direction. I realize that Ben did not say *he's* a Christian. It's possible he's not—every family has a black sheep—but this is the closest I've gotten to a date mentioning anything that remotely resembles a faith like mine, a family like mine and, basically, my number-one non-negotiable on my list of non-negotiables. Finally, The World's Best Dating Service seems to be listening.

I tell Ben more about my experience in Prague, my family and why I love teaching. We talk sports, politics and life in Orange County. Our banter is easy, we laugh a lot and even get caught checking each other out a few times. Before I know it, two-and-a-half hours later, I begin to notice the wait staff placing chairs on tops of tables and sweeping floors. I've barely touched my pasta because our conversation has been nonstop. When we get up to leave, Ben leads me out the door with his hand on my back. He grabs my valet ticket from me. *Is he really paying for my valet?* Yes, he is. *So, Ben, are you busy for the rest of your life? Because I'd like to spend the rest of mine with you.* If only I had the courage to say things like that maybe I could have saved myself a small fortune on a year of blind dates. On second thought, those lines only work in the movies; in real life, they're disasters. Thankfully, I use some self-control, slip Ben my number and give him a quick hug as my car pulls up. Before I get in, I take one more look. He's actually a lot taller than I realized, and these golden flats are my new favorite shoes.

* * * *

A few days after the wonderful date with Ben, my mind was full of possibilities. Why is it that we girls can't just think about today? I catch myself thinking about what my family will think of him, what our kids might look like (hoping that my tall genes would overpower his short genes), and where our house with the white picket fence will be.

Date number one was on a Monday night, and by Wednesday, we had plans for date number two. Ben wanted to take me to dinner and asked me to pick the restaurant. I am pretty traditional when it comes to dating and prefer the man to have a plan; but if that's what Ben thought was best, that was okay with me. "This way, I'll know what kind of place you like and can wow you on our third date," he said. *He's already thinking of our third date . . . I bet he has our honeymoon destination picked out as well!*

Ben says he'll pick me up at 5:30 on Thursday. We have decided on an early dinner because Ben plays on a recreational hockey team and they have a 9:00 game that night. Ben on the ice with a stick and a puck—very hot indeed. I decide to take Ben to one of my favorite restaurants along the coast. As we're driving to the restaurant, I remember that the last time I was there was with my ex-boyfriend. Remember "Colorado Chris"? *What was I thinking in bringing Ben here?* I was thinking about almond praline pie, one of my most favorite desserts at the restaurant. I was thinking about the romantic patio with the large fireplace. I was thinking about walking around town hand in hand after our dinner. I had forgotten all about the ex at this point.

It's a crisp fall night, and we're seated on the patio, close to the fireplace. Perfect. As we wait for our food to arrive, Ben suggests that we ask each other random questions . . . it's one of his favorite ways to get to know someone. He goes first. "What does your dad call you?"

"Why do you want to know that?" I ask, a bit defensively.

"I think it says a lot about a woman. Especially one who has a good relationship with her dad, like you seem to." Ben defends his question and slips in a compliment. *Nice work, Ben.*

I hesitate; I'm reluctant to reveal that my dad calls me "Princess." I can only imagine what conclusions he'll come to when he knows my nickname. If my dad calls me "Princess" that must imply I'm spoiled, or that I whine, have expensive taste, want all the attention . . . basically that I'm high maintenance. I loathe the "high maintenance" moniker most Orange County women are pegged with.

My brothers believe that every woman fits somewhere on the high maintenance scale. Some are "high-high," most are "high-medium" and then there are those few women who are "high-low" and make the rest of us look bad. Of course, all women are high maintenance from a man's standpoint! Just because we shower each day, prefer sit-down restaurants over drive-thrus and want more than two pairs of shoes (so impractical, I know) we're high maintenance. Whatever.

"My dad calls me 'Princess,'" I say quickly and a bit under my breath.

Ben laughs. I find myself going into far too much explanation as to why it really does not say much about me at all. "I don't think I'm high maintenance," I say with certainty. *Well, maybe a little; I'm a high medium.* "I don't whine (*not all that often*) and I don't have expensive taste (*at least not across the board*).

My turn. "Why did you join The World's Best Dating Service?" I ask with a smile and a raised brow. I can ask the hard questions too.

Ben, not one to shy away, jumps right in. "Well, I am not the kind of guy who is willing to ask for a girl's number at a bar. And to be honest, I don't think I want a girl who wants to be picked up in a bar."

"So what kind of girl are you looking for?" *Come back, words, please come back! Stupid, stupid, stupid!*

"An old-fashioned girl."

"Old-fashioned!?!" I don't hold back my surprise.

"Yeah, that is how you were described by the dating service."

"Hold on! They describe me as OLD-FASHIONED. So what were you envisioning? A bun? Long corduroy skirt? Clogs with knee socks? Yikes! I am impressed that you were willing to even meet me!" I totally miss the bigger point here. He pretty much said he's looking for someone like me, but I am so stunned by "old-fashioned" that it goes right over my head.

"Don't worry, I was pleasantly surprised when I saw you. In your case, old-fashioned is not a bad thing." He says it with a wink. I blush.

The questions continue like this throughout the evening. Since it's the week before Thanksgiving, we talk about our plans for the holiday and family traditions. The crisp air turns to a chill, Ben pays the bill and we head back to my place. He drops me off at my condo and gets out of the car to say good-bye.

It's at this point that Ben earns his nickname Besos—"kisses" in Spanish. I have a revelation: I like kissing a man that I can look directly in the eye. Very comfortable. I am not one to normally kiss on the second date. (Not that I have a "no kiss on the second date" policy. Since I don't go on many second dates, it has not been an issue.) However, this sweet kiss came very naturally.

The last thing Besos says is, "So, can we do this again next week?"

What? Kiss? Sure! Oh, you mean dinner? Of course!

"Yes, I'd love to," old-fashioned Megan replies.

"I'll call you. Have a great weekend."

I float up to my condo and have sweet dreams about Besos that night.

* * * *

About five days after our second date, and with only one day before Thanksgiving, Besos called. Actually, he returned my call. I know, all the laws of traditional dating state that the man is supposed to chase the woman, but I just could not resist. *What was he doing? Was he thinking about me?* A phone call was harmless I told myself. Besos called the next night. From the start it sounded obligatory.

"So, I got your message. How are you?" Ben asks without great enthusiasm.

"I'm great. How about you? Did you have a good weekend? What did you do?" *Stop with the questions, Megan.* Poor guy, he probably felt interrogated.

We talk for about three minutes when he says, "I gotta run . . . I have a game. Happy Thanksgiving!"

"Um, bye," I manage to get out. Silence. Did he just hang up with out saying good-bye?

Thanks to that phone call, there is now a nice little dent in my kitchen wall where the phone landed when I threw it. I was mad. Mad at myself, because after two dates I had already developed unrealistic expectations of what Besos and I were. For all I knew, he had spent his weekend on dates with other girls. That's the nature of the beast called a dating service. Besos would meet other women; I would meet other men. I knew very well what I was getting myself into, but still, I wanted Besos to want ME! One word: overreaction.

I take a moment to compose myself, pick up my phone off the floor and decide to go for a run. It always seems to clear my head. The next morning, I head to San Diego for Thanksgiving, all the while working to get Besos out of my head; but honestly, he was never too far from my mind.

Monday afternoon after the Thanksgiving holiday.

Text message received: "Megan, just returned from my trip. How was your turkey day? Ben."

It's been seven days, and Besos is back in touch!!!! I am back in the game. I ♥ Thanksgiving! We send a few texts back and forth and the perma-smile returns to my face. (Yes, I am the girl whose mood hinges on a man. Yes, I realize this can be a problem. Yes, God and I are working on it and I can happily say I am in recovery.)

The next day Besos sends another text asking me to dinner that very night. Dilemma: I've made plans to get a Christmas tree with my roommate, and my Bible study group is coming over.

A confession: I have an unhealthy desire to not become "that girl." We all know her—the one who drops all her friends when a guy enters the picture. The one who makes him her life. The one who somehow manages to fit him into every conversation.

"You drive a Toyota?! That's crazy, so does Ben!"

"You have a sister?! You won't believe this, but so does Ben!"

"You brush your teeth?! No way, so does _____!" (Fill in the blank with whatever man is in the picture.)

It's Christmas trees, Allison and God for me tonight. Sorry, Besos!

Message Sent: "Bummer, I have plans for tonight! Maybe later in the week? Megan."

Message Received: "My loss. That's what I get for asking last minute! I'll call you."

Five days pass and no Ben. Disappointed? Yes. Frustrated? Yes. Giving up? No. But before I make my next move, I need some moral support and advice from someone who will shoot straight with me. I call my younger brother.

"Drewbie. Hi, it's Megs."

"Hey, Megs, what's up?"

"I need some advice . . ."

I tell him the whole story.

And then I finally get to the point. "Is it too forward for me to text Besos and see if he wants to get together for dinner this week? Just a little kick in the pants to let him know I am still interested?"

"Text him? I hate to break it to you, Megan, but your text is not going to change God's plan." He's so right.

Moments later: "Ben, Hope you're doing well. I'd love to get together this week if you're available. Talk to you soon. Megan"

Message sent. Since people always have their phones on them and rarely miss a text or a call, if you don't hear back in an instant, you did not make the cut. Essentially you've been wait listed. They'll just get back to you whenever. So when Besos did not respond immediately, I, of course, fell back into full panic mode.

The next night I get my response. Besos calls and the first words out of his mouth are, "You must think I am the biggest jerk."

"Well, not the biggest, but . . ."

Besos laughs. "I'm sorry, I've just been really busy with work. And . . . I . . . leaving . . . week . . . sport."

"What? You're breaking up . . . say that again."

Phone goes dead.

Message received: "I'm in a bad zone. I'll call you tomorrow. I promise."

Unfortunately, Besos's bad zone led to what I call the "Besos Breakdown." You guessed it, Besos kissed me good-bye. He never called back. If I am totally honest, I admit I really wanted to see him again, and again, and again. I sincerely wanted to date Besos. There were so many things I liked about him, and after two dates there was a great deal more that I wanted to learn.

So I sulked; slept with my phone in case he called at, let's say, 2:00 A.M.; finished two cartons of mint chocolate chip ice cream in two days and fell prey to some retail therapy. And then (maybe two weeks later . . . I know, pathetic) I eventually came to my senses and snapped out of it. I realized there'd be another guy, and I'd better focus on meeting him. But I did have a few things I wanted to say to Besos. I penned this is my journal the night I let Besos go:

> *Besos, it's not my fault that I have cankles.* I know they are not attractive, but just like your height, there is nothing I can do about it. And, I'm not going to dye my hair. If you want a blonde, there are plenty of bottle blondes in Orange County to choose from. Furthermore, I like the five extra pounds I am carrying around because when I bump into things, I am well padded. I am me. Take it or leave it. I am far past the point (PRAISE THE LORD!) of thinking that if I was just this or that I'd have a man. So I get it, you're not interested. God has different plans for me. You lose, and I've moved on. You do have different plans for me, right, God? I know it's all about Your timing and not mine, but can I make a friendly suggestion that we speed things up a bit?*

---

*Cankles: what you get when your ankles are swallowed by your calves.

Kiddo

About the time I joined The World's Best Dating Service, it started raining men. My dating life is best described as feast or famine, and during the warm months of autumn, I found myself happily at a feast. I'm talking "two dates a week" feast. And not just from the dating service. People came out of the woodwork wanting to set me up with their friends, their sons, their child's teacher, even their doctor (yes, please—if he is under 35). When people say, "I have someone I want you to meet," I usually respond with, "I'm always up for a thoughtful setup." Emphasis on "thoughtful"—my way of letting them know that just because their friend, son or doctor is single with a pulse doesn't mean we're a "match made in heaven." On second thought, a single doctor with a pulse would be perfect.

After signing up for The World's Best Dating Service, I was slightly hesitant to agree to setups via friends. Why? These introductions were free. I had paid good money to meet a man via the dating service and I'd be a little bitter if one of these freebies worked! All that hard-earned cash down the dating drain. (Yeah, I am sure I'd get over it as soon as I fell in love with a freebie!)

One such setup was via my friend Abigail. She wanted me to meet Adam, a guy she was in a Bible study with. He was also a teacher and lived right down the street from me. Abigail is a very picky dater, so I trusted that this was a "thoughtful setup." Through the course of our friendship we've spent countless hours talking about men. Like me, she is not into shorter guys even though she herself is only five foot four. "If he's short, how would he put up the Christmas lights?" She asks in all seriousness.

"Um, it's called a ladder. Even tall men use them when putting up Christmas lights," I sarcastically reply. Ideally she wants a man that tops out at about six feet. I tell her that she could go a lot shorter and things would still be fine. Selfishly, I want her to go for shorter men so we're not fishing in the same pond. *Leave the tall men for me, please!*

"It just seems like a pain. Life would be so much easier with a tall man," Abigail laments.

"Now you're just making excuses. Watch; God is going to have you fall in love with someone who is five foot six. But don't worry, I will get you a ladder as a wedding gift."

"And you'll find a man who is five foot eight and be forced to eBay all your high heels in order to buy flats. And you'll still be taller than him."

We both burst out laughing to cover the fact that we really have no idea who God has for us and our mates quite possibly won't match what we've envisioned for ourselves. Ultimately it is out of our hands. It is in God's hands, and honestly, deep down, I am so glad He's in charge, and not me.

Abigail was a current client of Match.com (as was Adam) so she let me do some snooping on her account to check him out. (Of course I Googled him as well—Google is a girl's best friend when it comes to getting dirt on potential dates, but Match had much better info.) AdammeetsEve (his profile name, which I thought was rather cute) made a good first impression. I learned that he loved Elvis music, played the guitar and counted Netflix as one of the best inventions of the twenty-first century. His picture showed him in a baseball cap and sunglasses, but Abigail vouched for the fact that he was cute. I gave Abigail the go-ahead to pass on my number.

Adam called me on a Thursday afternoon. I remember thinking he was easy to talk to and the conversation did not have too many strange silences. We chatted about home ownership and how much we liked our little slice of suburbia. I learned that he enjoys Mexican food, travels whenever he can and does not have cable. He's trying to reduce his carbon footprint, so "getting rid of cable" was part of that plan. However, he was getting his TV fix by watching all 11 seasons of *Cheers* via Netflix. *Interesting*. I try to do the math in my head. Eleven seasons of *Cheers* . . . 20+ shows a season at 30 minutes each . . . that's a lot of time spent watching what I consider to be a mediocre TV show. Now if it was *Grey's Anatomy* or *30 Rock* that would be another story. (I've done the math. We're talking at least 110 hours.) Adam is not particularly inquisitive about me, but I figure he will ask me questions on our date.

Toward the end of the conversation, he says, "So, what are you doing this weekend?"

"I'm actually headed out of town on Saturday morning to visit my brother and his wife," I say.

"How do you feel about walks?"

Um, well, I like going on walks . . . what kind of question is this? I think.

"Walks are great," I say.

"Well, it's been really hot lately, do you want to meet me for a walk on Saturday morning? How about 7:00 A.M.?"

"Sure, why not." What happened to a traditional first date of coffee or ice cream? I normally sleep in on Saturday, but the sleeping-in excuse is right up there with "I need to wash my hair," and I don't think Adam merits that line . . . yet. Why did I agree to do this? Well, why not? It is something different, and this way I will get my daily workout in as well. Actually, I think

I agreed because I'm in the Blind Date Zone. Throw a blind date at me—I can handle it. I'm invincible, untouchable. A walk seemed pretty harmless and could be a lot of fun.

Adam and I meet in a Starbucks parking lot halfway between our two condos. I figured it was him because he was parked away from the other cars and leaning on the side of a new Prius. *He's taking this carbon footprint thing seriously!* Baggy shorts, baggy shirt, baseball cap and aviator glasses. Those sunglasses and baseball cap looked familiar—they were the same ones he was wearing in the Match.com photo. I'm wearing navy workout shorts, a tank top, deodorant and mascara.

I park next to him and hop out of my car. When I greet him, I take off my sunglasses, with the hope that he would do the same. Just a common courtesy, right? Adam says, "Hey, there," and shakes my hand. Sunglasses firmly in place on his face.

He suggests we get some water from Starbucks before we get started. Good idea. *Okay, we're going inside; I'll get to see what this guy looks like.* Maybe this Starbucks was particularly bright, or Adam is famous and I don't know it, but he kept his sunglasses on. Water in hand, we exit and I start walking in the direction of a trail about 300 yards away.

"Let's go this way," he says pointing in the direction of a huge hill.

"It's too early for hills, Adam, this way is easier," I say with a chuckle, playfully grabbing his arm and pulling him in my direction.

"Here's the route we're going to take," he says, shaking free from my grip. He reaches into his pocket and pulls out a hand drawn map of our area. Sure enough, all the major streets are labeled and there are little pairs of footprints along the route he planned for us to take. While this is slightly over the top, I do appreciate that Adam had really thought about our date and where we're headed. *No problem, I'll suck it up and face the hills.*

Very early into our walk, we reach our first signal. As we stand at the streetlight, waiting to cross, he says, "So, kiddo, what kind of music do you like?" I turn around, assuming a kid has rolled up on his bike. No kid to be found. *Really? He's talking to me? Really? He just called me kiddo? Okay. Well, this just got a bit more interesting.*

I was so taken aback by being called "kiddo" that I can't even remember how I answered the question. I have nothing against nicknames, or pet names for that matter, but on a first date, I find it strange. We keep walking. I'm really not sure what to do. Should I ask him if he forgot my name? Do I refer to him as "dude" the rest of the date? Do I just let it go? It had only happened once, so I figured it was not a big deal. There are much worse things he could be calling me, so maybe I could live with "kiddo."

Unfortunately, this was not a one-time occurrence. I was "kiddo" for the next two hours. Yes, I said two hours. Two long, hot hours of walking and talking. Adam shared how he used to be a runner but had recently hurt his leg and was now only able to walk. He complained about some of his students and asked me to share my favorite lesson plan. Was he going to take notes on my best practices in the classroom? Then he asked me to share one of the funniest things that has happened in my classroom. Since these questions required long answers, I figured this would be a perfect opportunity to try speaking in the third person. A sneaky way to remind him I had a first name.

"One of the units I teach in Geography is on Africa. I spent a couple of days talking about apartheid in South Africa and Nelson Mandela. I showed my students some photographs of Mandela's house and Soweto Township. When I asked if any of my students were familiar with Nelson Mandela, one of my freshman girls raised her hand and let out a squeal. 'I have, Ms. Carson! Tyra Banks took all the models there on *America's Next Top Model*. I had no idea that he was a real person!' *Great*, I

thought, *my students are learning more geography from Tyra than me.*
I had to turn around and face the whiteboard to stop from
laughing. I did not want to laugh at her face. I said to myself,
Megan, you have to stop laughing."
   Did you hear that, Adam? Megan, my name is Megan. M-E-G-A-N.
"That's a good story, kiddo." *Good, but apparently not good
enough, because you're still not using my name. I give up. It's a lost
cause.* I was not willing to give it another shot because I didn't
want to become the date that talked in the third person. However, I did use Adam's name multiple times to try to get him to
use mine, but that did not work either.
   Our walk included a stop to check out his chalk drawings
that he apparently had completed the day before: rainbows, fish
and a hopscotch course. There was no explanation of these drawings. *Did he create these all by himself? Does he baby-sit in the evenings
to earn some extra cash? Was it some sort of test to see if I'd hop down the
hopscotch squares?* I did not ask . . . I did not care. Three times he
asked me, "So, are you having fun? What do you think, are you
having a good time?"
   Honestly, Adam, I don't think so. Actually, no, I am not having a good time. You are unique (read: odd, strange, a few bricks
short of a load) and I want to go home.
   We round the final corner of the trail and off in the distance
I can see our cars, "The Promised Land!" A patch of asphalt
never looked so good. *I could kiss that asphalt I am so happy to see it.*
My water was long gone, I dripped with perspiration and I had
not heard my own name in hours.
   "You know, I find a girl who owns her own condo to be
really sexy." *Oh, boy. Who uses the words "condo" and "sexy" in the
same sentence?*
   Awkward laugh. He continues.
   "I just think it's great that you're independent and have your
own place and a good job."

I'm silent. We reach the Prius, and I know it's coming.

"So, do you want to go out again?"

"No thanks, kiddo. You are creepy, and chalk drawings are not sexy."

Run to car, hop in and drive away.

Why do I always think of the best thing to do after the fact, Megan?!

Instead, I said something like, "It was nice meeting you, but I just am not interested in seeing you again."

"Okay, bye," he chokes out.

That's when he ran to his car, jumped in and drove away. Not kidding. He ran. I wanted to yell, "It's not polite to run . . . and . . . I thought you were injured!" I got into my car and just sat there for a moment. This dating adventure has provided far too many "Did that just happen?" moments, and this was absolutely one of them. Thankfully, I responded not with tears but laughter. In the end, I never saw what Adam really looked like because he rocked the hat and sunglasses the entire time. For all I know, he's got a unibrow and the beginnings of a mullet.

Thanks a lot, Abigail! By the way, I have a friend I want to set you up with . . . and he's only five foot four!!!

. . . .

8

The Others

Once the dating service got into full swing and I started to become less inept in this whole dating thing, I got over the "freebie" phobia. I took an "all hands on deck" approach. Before signing up with The World's Best Dating Service, when someone (a stranger, neighbor, family friend, dentist) asked if I had a boyfriend, my standard response was, "No," and then I would quickly change the subject. But with my recent confidence, courtesy of The World's Best, my new response was, "No, but do you know anybody?"

Before long, I was being set up with successful sons, single brothers, even my friend's ex-boyfriend (yeah, don't go there, ladies). One woman even offered to be my Yenta. I had my very own Jewish matchmaker—free of charge. She was a realtor by day and in the end did a better job of helping me find a condo than a man. Like my setup with "Kiddo," these men came free, and better yet, with a recommendation.

My Mark

The McCroskey Matchmaking Service (my roommate's parents) contacted me with a great idea. They had a stellar Christian guy they wanted me to meet. They described him as six foot eight . . . *SOLD . . . say no more.* He also played college basketball, had a close-knit family and a great sense of humor. And he was a golfer. *"I do."*

Within days of first hearing about Mark, the McCroskeys wasted no time in arranging a meet-up. Allison and I were to meet her parents and Mark at church and then afterwards go to breakfast. This was my first church date (as well as my first date with chaperones), and I looked forward to worshiping with Allison, her parents and Mark. As Allison and I entered the sanctuary, it was easy to spot Mark—he stood high above the crowd. Allison had told me he was very good-looking; she was right.

As we sat there in the worship service it was easy to be attracted to Mark, even though all we had said was hello. Not much is sexier than a man who loves God and is not afraid to show it. *This is what I want in a relationship!* Of course there was a chance that Mark was not The One, but this moment sitting next to him was a much-needed reminder that I still wanted God's best, and that was a man committed to a relationship with Him.

As the music ended and the pastor began to preach, my mind began to wander. *What will I have for breakfast? Gosh, he smells good. I wonder if I can squeeze in a nap before date number two.* My mental wandering came to a halt when I heard an audible voice say, "It's not him." *Excuse me? What was Pastor Doug talking about?* I look around and realize this voice was not coming from the pulpit. I was too embarrassed to ask Allison if she had heard it, but there was no denying the fact that *I* had heard it. Now, I do talk to myself (*all intelligent people do*), but I rarely hear voices. And I am not one who hears an audible voice from God, but there was no refuting it . . . God was talking to me.

But not to worry, right? "It's not him" could have been referring to my second date later in the day, with "Dr. Dirk." Certainly, God was not referring to the gorgeous tall drink of water sitting next to me. *Whew . . . good thing I am going on two dates today, or this would be a huge bummer! Oh, and by the way, God, why are You speaking to me now when the* other *men were clearly "not him" and You said nothing? Answer me that!*

Somehow I get my mind back on the sermon, and when the service ends, Mark and I head to the patio with the McCroskeys trailing behind us. We all chat for a short while about the sermon and the beautiful weather. We all agree we're hungry and should head to Molly's for pancakes and their signature *huevos rancheros*. Breakfast was good—both the food and conversation. We laughed a lot and I was able to be myself, considering Mark and I had three chaperones.

Throughout the meal, Allison kept smiling at me as if to say, "You're doing great, keep it up," like I was a beginner at this or something. Her parents made sure to fill in the gaps on stories they were telling about people they all knew but I had never heard of. I left breakfast excited about the possibility of seeing Mark again. Not only was he easy on the eyes, but he also seemed to be as wonderful as the McCroskeys had said. High five McCroskey Matchmaking Service! (*I wonder if I can transfer my subscription over from The World's Best Dating Service?*)

On the ride home, Allison and I recapped the date, and Mark received his nickname: "My Mark." I don't even know where it came from, but it was rooted in schoolgirl-like hopefulness: dreams of seeing him in between classes, anticipating how he would ask me to the prom, envisioning me wearing his letterman's jacket. All those things I never had in high school but wanted. Of course, I would never wear Mark's letterman's jacket, but maybe his sweater that he'd leave behind in my car. As my heart fluttered, I realized I had already developed a full-blown crush.

Unfortunately, as it turns out, this nickname was a bit presumptuous considering there was no contact after our "date." Apparently, God *was* speaking to me about Mark. Within a few months of meeting me, he reconciled with his ex-girlfriend and they are now happily married.

But all was not lost. In addition to meeting a man that I felt an instant connection with, this date served as a very important reminder. In the haze of meeting bachelors #1, #2, #3 and more, there were moments, days, weeks even when I veered off course. Times when I tried to talk myself into someone; pep talks I'd rehearse over less-than-stellar candidates. Yes, I wanted (and needed) dating experience, but I was coming dangerously close to a point where I was willing to date someone if they were male and breathing. Why was I even considering someone who only *might* be interested in a relationship with God? Who had I become? What was I thinking? It was time to reevaluate. I needed to get down on my knees and do what I like to call a "Hello, God, it's me, Megan" moment. Back to my first love.

Lord, thank You that You give me what I need when I need it. Meeting Mark was a necessary reminder that I can't do this without You. I don't want to do this without You! I am not Your assistant; You don't need my help. Instead, You want me to seek You first in all things, believing that You're in control.

When I returned home from the date with "My Mark," I was on cloud nine. In my mind, he had met my parents, proposed and it was days before the wedding. I had skipped from A to Z, forgetting that none of this would become a reality if he didn't ask me out again. *Oh, that's right, he never did.*

Put your game face on, Megan. You have another date in less than three hours.

Dr. Dirk

Dr. Dirk came with quite a recommendation from some close friends. He was their family doctor, had a great bedside manner and looked adorable in scrubs. The matchmakers had exchanged cell phone pictures for us, and he looked pretty cute on a two-by-two-inch screen. I knew very little about Dirk before I met him, less than what the dating service tells me, and moments before the date, I started to panic. What if it's him? Not a "Ohh, I hope it's him!" but more of a "Oh, please, God, I don't think I want it to be him." I had just met "My Mark" and was still denying God's message. Dirk? What kind of name is that! (*Oh, that's right, one I've made up. Nonetheless, his real name was not one you'd want to have to repeat the rest of your life. "This is my husband, Dirk." "Dirt?" "No, Dirk." "Kirk?" "Oh, forget it."*)

Earlier in the week, we tried to have a pre-date, "get to know you" conversation but spoke to each other's voicemail repeatedly instead. We did, however, set up a time and place for our date. Initially, Dirk wanted the date to be a surprise and asked if he could reserve me for an entire day. *The whole day . . . yikes!* I casually talked him out of that pretty quickly. I prefer the two-hour max first meeting. Get a little info and leave (hopefully) wanting more. The Dr. wanted to pick me up at home, also a no-no on a first date, especially a blind date. I prefer a getaway car. But he insisted. I said yes and then called our matchmaker to see if it was safe for me to ride in the car with him. I know, too many episodes of *Dateline*. She laughed and gave me the go-ahead.

Flash forward to Sunday evening. Dirk arrives at my condo and I am greeted with a big bouquet of flowers and a mouth full of braces. The flowers, of course, were beautiful and very thoughtful, but the braces were not what I expected. I know some of us discover the orthodontist later in life, and that it's still a privilege for many people to be called "brace face." In Dirk's case, mom and dad didn't pay for braces. (Thanks, Bruce and Karen!) Though, even with the braces, he made a good first impression. He was well dressed and handsome.

Dirk escorted me to his car and opened my door. Love that! While driving to dinner Dirk told me that Plan A (had I been game for the all-day date) was Medieval Times! *Oh, man! Dirk, dude, you don't take a girl, let alone on a first date, to a place where you eat with your fingers, wear silly crowns and watch dirty horses run around in a circle. Maybe for a six-year-old's birthday, but certainly not for a first date.*

"Too bad that didn't work out," I say, holding back my true feelings.

"Yeah, let's keep it in mind for the second date."

No need to be overly confident, Dr. Dirk! Instead, I laugh.

Dirk asks me about exercising (he's into martial arts and box-ing), and I tell him about my running adventures. I love to run but had been in a bit of a slump because of a foot injury (and sulk-ing over bad dates). He lets out a cackle, rubs his hands together and cracks his knuckles. Mind you, he's still driving. "I'm sure it's nothing I can't handle," he claims with too much *machismo.*

You're scaring me, Dirk. Eyes on the road, please. And you're get-ting nowhere near my feet.

We arrive at dinner, order margaritas and fish tacos and start in on the chips and salsa. Conversation is easy, mainly because I am doing all the listening. *Man, this guy can talk!* I begin to space out. *What am I going to wear to work tomorrow? I wonder what "My Mark" is doing?*

"So do you like dirt bike riding?" Dirk asks.

Um, Dirk, did you notice my pearls?

"You know, I've never been, so I don't know. How about you?" This was the first question he had asked in quite some time and I should have run with it by saying something like, "I love dirt bike riding!"

"We should go sometime! Are you free next weekend?" he says with a wink. A wink. One of the most misunderstood facial expressions known to man. This could mean, "Just kidding" or "You're cute" or "You think I'm kidding, but I am quite serious. Come away with me for the weekend." Knowing that the good Dr. was a Christian, I took the wink as "You're cute and I am just being a bit flirty."

Thirty minutes later I knew more about dirt bike riding than I ever wanted to know. Even though Orange County is filled with Hollywood wannabes, too much plastic (American Express or otherwise) and more luxury cars than most countries in the world, there is a large population of OC residents that love dirt biking. They hitch their camper and bike trailer to their Mercedes SUV, somehow manage to squeeze through the gates of their posh community and hit the 91 freeway east to get the heck out of Dodge and get their off-road on. I have students who are actually sponsored in this sport. Guys *and* girls who are paid to dirt bike ride! It's a mystery to me . . . or it was before I got a tutorial from Dirk. He's thinking of refocusing his medical practice to cater specifically to dirt bike riders. *Really? You could make a living treating dirt bike riders?* Maybe I should call him Dr. Dirt Bike or Dr. Dirk Bike. (*Ha. I crack myself up!*)

Conversation comes to a lull, and even with the aid of a Diet Coke, I am fading fast. I excuse myself to the restroom, and when I return to the table, Dirk has paid the bill. As we head out of the restaurant, Dirk grabs my hand. Okay . . . not what I was expecting, but at this point, it would be rude to pull away. I figure it's a few more steps to the car where the handholding will naturally stop. I climb into his truck and begin to fumble with the contents of my purse to keep my hands occupied and unavailable.

"What do you want to do next?" Dirk asks. I want to go home. I am exhausted. While the dinner with Dirk was interesting, I am mentally spent. And poor Dirk, he does not realize that only hours earlier I met someone I am planning on marrying. He really did not stand a chance tonight. And I did not give him a chance. That's 100 percent my fault.

"I don't know, what sounds good to you?" My noncommittal response opens the door for him to choose, maybe not a good idea.

"I know a good coffee place in San Clemente."

Yikes, more time in the car. "Why don't we hit a coffee spot closer to my place?" He agrees and we land at a Starbucks in my neighborhood—one that has been the scene of previous dates.

It's comfortable and very close to home if I need to make a quick exit.

At coffee I learn that Dirk really likes Legos and skateboarding. Unfortunately, I have checked out at this point and can barely make it through my chai tea. Dirk senses that I am fading and offers to take me home. I struggle to keep my eyes open during the five-minute drive to my condo complex. When we arrive, Dirk insists on walking me to my doorstep. As we're headed up the stairs to my place, he asks what I am doing tomorrow.

"I have the day off of work and am really looking forward to relaxing!" I say.

"Would you want to meet for breakfast?" he asks.

"I don't think so, I really just want to keep the day open," I say in the nicest way possible.

"Lunch or dinner, maybe?"

With a little more force I say, "That's nice of you, but I am hoping to just chill all day."

"Well, I have a boxing class tomorrow night, wanna come?" Dirk offers as a last-ditch attempt.

DR. DIRK! PAGING, DR. DIRK! You just don't get it, do you? I am sorry, but I don't want to see you tomorrow.

"How about you call me later in the week and we'll see if we can find another time to hang out. Good night," I say with one foot already in the door.

Dirk gives me a wave and I close the door behind me. I'll admit it was not the smoothest good-bye on my part. And I could have given Dirk a break and seen him the next day, but he was overwhelming to me. I sensed that I had made a bigger impression on him than he had on me. His forwardness caused me to want to run away . . . I mean back away.

I throw down my purse and sit on the couch next to Allison. Ever the listening friend, she gets an earful about Dr. Dirk. As I detail the quirks and missteps of my date, a cloud of sadness sweeps over me. I'm embarrassed by my critical breakdown of Dr. Dirk. Has this become a game to me? Do I not realize that these men are human, imperfect and just being themselves? Am I that catty girl who is looking for perfection when she in fact brings more junk to the table than some of the men she meets? On this night, my do-you-really-want-to-say-this-filter has malfunctioned and I admit all of this to Allison. She reminds me that I lead with my heart. It's okay for me to trust my gut, but I need to be sure I am giving these men a fair shot. While I might overuse pro/con lists, in the end, it's my heart that makes most of the decisions. This gives me plenty to think about. I hug her goodnight and head to bed.

Before falling asleep, I pen the following in my journal:

Lord, I know it comes as no surprise to You that I'm afraid I have developed a terrible habit (?), tendency (?), superpower (?) to assume, think or believe that You will have The One be someone that has a quirk or characteristic or name that will drive me crazy, but eventually I will have to learn to love it. I fear that in order to spite me (because even though You tell me my sins are forgiven, I see scarlet, not white) You will have me marry some weirdo, because that is all that will be left or that's all that will have me. I fear becoming a spinster. It runs in my family, on both sides. And it skips a generation, and my generation is next up. I know that these are very irrational fears (along with dying surrounded by cats and wine bottles) but they sometimes (okay, oftentimes) motivate my thinking. Dirk had plenty of quirks. But so do I! He was a very nice guy and he deserved a second date, but I got anxious because of my irrational thoughts. Obviously I have a lot to learn and need to work on giving grace. But first I know I need to accept Your grace or this will never work.

Lord, You also know that I love You and am daily growing to trust Your hands in my life. It's not easy and I have moments of pure terror and pure peace. You have proven to be faithful in my life, and will continue to be. My head knows better than my heart, my heart just gets very confused sometimes. I desperately want it to "feel" right when I meet someone. That "you will know when you know" feeling. I am realizing that everyone deserves a chance. I would want someone to give me a chance. God, let me see these men as You see them. Not as who I want them to be, or imagine they should be. I just have one small request: please make sure that my man, wherever he is, buys a map or asks for directions sooner than later because he is obviously lost. The sooner the better, because I've started shopping for cats. And one cat will need a friend, and that is a very slippery slope. I love You. Thank You for loving me.

9

Cheeks

. . . .

I took a short break from dating after "The Others." The tiresome rigors of "Kiddo" and "Dr. Dirk" combined with the disappointment of things not moving forward with "Besos" or "My Mark" were more than I had bargained for just three months into my year of blind dates. I needed time to regroup and refocus. I had paid for a full year of dates, but if I met someone or needed a break, I could put my subscription on hold for up to a year. I did not feel the need to officially put a hold on my matches, but I waited a full two weeks before calling my matchmaker back when she left a voicemail about Kyle.

A small part of me was hopeful that The World's Best Dating Service had forgotten about me. No such luck. Kyle would be my eighth blind date in three months. This was record-breaking for me. My heart was numbed by the shock of it all. I had my moments of seriously questioning why I was doing this to myself— the anticipation, nerves, disappointments, emotional highs and lows. It felt like a cruel form of torture. First dates can be worse than a trip to the dentist. Who would agree to go to the dentist 20 times in one year? *But if the dentist was cute and single . . .*

I agreed to meet Kyle for dinner in a city halfway between the two of us. It was a cold Sunday, and I had spent most of the afternoon in pajamas, catching up on TiVo. The last thing I wanted to do was get dressed up and head out to meet man number nine, most likely Mr. McWrong. *Megan, with that attitude, you'll get nowhere!* Since canceling on Kyle was not an option, I needed to get myself off the couch and into something more attractive than pajamas.

Now, I consider myself a pretty stylish person. I was even voted most stylish teacher where I work. But if my wardrobe were a pie chart, the breakdown would be the following: 35 percent Banana Republic (all the work basics), 35 percent J.Crew (all the weekend basics) and 20 percent Nordstrom (shoes, shoes, shoes). The remaining 10 percent is a little bit of everything else, mainly things I liked on the mannequin that sit in my closet for months with the tags still on. Most days I have no problem putting together a great ensemble. However, some days I look more TJ Maxx and less J.Crew. I love a good trip to TJ Maxx, but I often find things that kinda work but were better left on the rack. My closet can be the same thing.

As I am running out the door, I ask Allison, "Does this look okay?"

"Umm . . . what kind of look are you going for?"

"One level above 'I don't care.'"

"Done. Actually more 'soccer mom who is one level above I don't care.'"

Perfect.

Kyle was described as a self-starter who loves adventure, challenges and meeting new people. You would think the dating service was trying to get him a job by the way they were pitching him to me. He lives in the Inland Empire, owns his own business and played baseball in high school. And . . . drum roll, please . . . he's five foot ten, one inch taller than me. So tonight I am wearing my leopard print flats. I'm a saucy soccer mom. I arrive at the restaurant and scan the dining room. No potential Kyles. No potentials, period. I march up to the host. He asks if I want to be seated. Why not?

We head to a nearby table that is small, round and appears to be illuminated. Yep, sure enough, when I sit down I realize that it's directly beneath one of their few and far between recessed lights. Kyle can't get here fast enough . . . I am desperate for some company so I don't look quite so, well, desperate. *Please come soon, Kyle. Save me from looking like the pathetic scene in a movie where the girl waits and waits and waits, and no one shows up.*

Normally, I don't have a problem being by myself. I like (and need) time alone. I don't hesitate to do something even if no one else will join me. I love going to the movies where my only company is popcorn and a Diet Coke. But sitting alone with a spotlight on me feels different. I am dressed up and clearly waiting for someone. I am overly self-conscious. My singleness feels very apparent. And then I notice the crayons on my table. At least I can look busy while looking desperate. I practice writing my name upside down, draw a self-portrait and beat myself at tic-tac-toe three times.

Twenty minutes under the spotlight and Kyle finally shows up. The host just points to me. *Thanks. Thanks a lot. It's rude to point, ya know!* Kyle walks over, and the first thing I notice are his cheeks—not the kind that young women want to squeeze, the kind your grandma wants to squeeze. Poor guy. My cankles and his cheeks. Deadly combination. I decide at this moment that if he is The One, we're adopting.

As Kyle walks over I am not sure whether to stand up and say "hi," put a hand out to shake his or what. Instead I go with the painfully lame "half stand" where I am neither sitting nor standing but squatting. I fumble with my menu to cover up the doodling that I've been doing the past 20 minutes. I put my hand out and he awkwardly shakes it. The only thing that could have made this moment worse would have been a dead fish handshake. Thankfully, Kyle had a good strong grip.

He sits down and lets out a sigh. "Traffic was miserable; I am so glad I am finally here. Let's eat." *Was that his way of apologizing for being 20 minutes late? Apology not accepted.* "Unfortunately, I have a surprise party to be at in about an hour; do you mind if we just get an appetizer?" That is the first positive thing about the night so far. Appetizer equals quick date.

Kyle and I continue to chat and I find out that we actually have a lot in common. Conversation is flowing, but I am not feeling any attraction or "spark." I know physical attraction can come later in a relationship, and it's only been a few minutes. Don't get me wrong, Kyle was not unattractive, but I just wasn't feeling it.

My brother Drew always tells me that I'd be better off with a guy I can sit on a bench and talk to for hours, not one that I want to make out with for hours. Um . . . what kind of version of crazy talk is this? Drew, come on . . . who doesn't want to sit on a bench and make out? His theory is that over time those hot and heavy make-out sessions fade, and if you can't talk to someone (your boyfriend or your spouse) you're in trouble. Okay, I'll admit he has a point.

It turns out that Kyle and I both enjoy travel, sports and time with our family. Kyle starts to share about his glory days on his high school baseball team. He played catcher, and his team went to the California state championships his junior year but, unfortunately, were beat in the final game. "I still hate the school that beat us," he says with enough disdain that I know he's serious. "Where did you go to high school?" he asks. I lie. For the simple reason that I attended "that school," the one he hates. Oh, and I now work at "that school." And my brother Keith played baseball at "that school" and likely shared the field with Kyle at some point. Those factors did not concern me as much as the realization that we were now separated by only a few degrees. I knew where this was headed and I did not want to play the name game. I still suffered from a bit of "dating serv-ice shame" and wanted to keep this whole adventure under wraps, at least with certain people. *Of course, that was before some-one offered me a book deal.*

I switch the topic to family. "What does your family think about you joining the dating service?"

"I don't know."

"What do you mean?" I ask cautiously.

"Do you mean, what do they think about me using a dating service? Oh, gosh, I would never tell them, or anyone else for that matter!" he says. And then with a hushed tone he goes on, "What would they think? It's just so . . . so desperate." *Excuse me? I un-derstand if you want to call yourself desperate, but please don't take me down with you. I am using that very same service, Cheeks!* He contin-ues, "I normally tell them everything, especially my mom. I am a bit of a mama's boy, but this is just too personal. Have you told your family?"

"Of course. I don't tell them everything, but I figure if I meet someone, they will find out eventually anyway."

"Not me. If I meet someone, I am just going to lie about the details."

I want to ask what scenarios he's come up with to cover for meeting via the dating service, but his cell phone interrupts us.

"It's my mom . . . I gotta take it." I go back to my doodling. But don't worry, I can doodle and eavesdrop at the same time. I am dialed into Kyle's side of the conversation. "Hi, Mom. Oh, just out to dinner with Jason (*liar!*) . . . sure I'll tell him you say 'hi' . . . it's been a great day . . . I went to breakfast this morning with the Johnsons, then watched football . . . I know, can you be-lieve the Chargers lost? . . ." Three minutes later, and I am still eavesdropping. Kyle just can't seem to say good-bye to Mama. The waiter delivers the check. A perfect cue that he'd better hang up.

"I love you too, Mom . . . I know, I promise . . . okay, I will call when I get home . . . you're the best . . . kisses." *Kisses?* Apparently this is code for good-bye.

"My mom calls me at 7:45 every night. If I don't pick up she'll be worried."

Kyle has an odd way of apologizing. I don't think it's too much to ask for him to say, "I'm sorry for taking a call on our date." Maybe "I'm sorry" is not in his vocabulary. Well, it's in mine . . . and at this point, he might hear it in the form of, "I am sorry, but I don't want to see you again, Kyle." We split the check—$8.75 including tax and tip. Cheapest and fastest date so far.

Kyle does walk me to my car and asks for my number. I hesitate for a moment and then give in. I have yet to not hand over my number when a man asks for it. Next to some of the other dates, Kyle was not that bad. If he does call, I will weigh my options and consider a second date. My mind was not made up, and I just can't bring myself to reject someone to his face. I prefer phone . . . or text.

Speaking of texts . . . Kyle sends me one a few days later wanting to know if I can meet him for dinner that very night. *What? Mom is not available, and now you're calling in the second string?* I know that is a little harsh, but I would rather be asked out a few days in advance and over the phone. Yes, I can be spontaneous; but not knowing Kyle, I can't tell if dinner with me is a time filler or something he really wants to do.

I know that you men (all three of you reading this book) are rolling your eyes, thinking that I should give him a break; he would not ask me to dinner unless he really wanted to see me. But remember, I am old-fashioned and prefer a little bit of notice and the courtesy of a phone call, not a text. Boys (in this case, mama's boys) text. Men call. I text back to let him know I am not available.

Kyle and I talk on the phone two times and text some before he attempts to ask me out on a second "date."

The invite comes via . . . you guessed it, a text. Actually, a mass text.

"Any and all are invited to my New Year's Party! 9:00 at my place."

Sorry, Kyle. I won't be there.

As you can guess, that was the end of it with "Cheeks." Looking back, I think he was a nice guy and had good intentions, but there was a disconnect. I wasn't so sure I wanted to see him again; and since the efforts he was putting forth weren't exactly one level above "I care," I brushed him off. A rookie mistake. But really, I don't think two or three or four more dates would have changed anything. Don't worry, Cheeks, your secret's safe with me. I promise not to tell anyone I met you.

10

No, Thanks

As the fall dating season came to a close, and the frenzy of the holidays finally passed, I decided to take a break from dating. I wasn't throwing in the towel; I was not going on dates with "God"; I was not dating myself. I just needed to be pulled out of the game for a bit. I was headed on a 17-day Antarctic adventure with my all-time favorite date, my dad, and I needed that time to get myself back into fighting shape (I mean, dating shape) both physically and mentally. I called The World's Best Dating Service and officially put my membership on hold. *See ya, suckers!*

When Dad and I return from our trip, I'm still single (surprise, surprise) and hesitant to get back in the game. Then I remember that New Year's Eve was just a month ago.

New Year's = Resolutions.

New Year's = Men who have decided that 2008 is the year to find a bride.

New Year's = New sign-ups for The World's Best Dating Service and fresh matches for Megan!

Put me in, coach, I'm ready to play!

I call the dating service and ask to be reinstated. Two days later, Sarah calls me. *Who is Sarah? What happened to the other ladies who keep setting me up? Stay positive—maybe fresh blood is what you need.*

"Megan, I have a great match for you . . ." She may be new, but she has the standard opening line down. "His name is Blake, and he's six foot six."

I like the new girl already. I like Blake already. He's athletic and he attended one of my rival high schools. After high school, he went to college out of state. He currently lives in Huntington Beach, is close to his family, and is looking for a serious relationship. His availability is next week—the thirteenth, fourteenth or fifteenth. Did she just say he's available on the fourteenth? Funny, I am available on that day as well, because . . . it's *Valentine's Day!* Blake either has guts or he's clueless. Okay, Blake, I'll match your courage and raise you one for a heart's day date.

"The fourteenth will work. Do you think he knows it's Valentine's Day?" I ask Sarah.

"Good question. He said he's available on that night, so I guess he does."

This will be my first Valentine's Day date . . . ever. A few years back, I was dating Colorado Chris on Valentine's, but since he lived out of state, we did not go out on that night. Most years, my Valentine's Day is spent with girlfriends in front of the TV; we dare not venture out into the social scene that night—too depressing. I am not saying this is bad, it's just not ideal. Not ideal at all. I'm hopeful this date with Blake will be the date that breaks the "Valentine's Day Curse" and inaugurates a plethora of Valentine's dates in the years to come.

"Let's see," says Sarah. "You live in Carson, he lives in Corona; so where should you meet?"

"No, my last name is Carson, and I thought he lived in Huntington Beach?" I politely correct her.

"Oh, you're right. Did I mention that I am new?" *Actually, I figured that one out on my own, Sarah.*

Sarah manages to make a dinner reservation for us at a swanky Italian place. I'm feeling good that I won't be spending Valentine's Day on the couch with Bridget Jones, Orville Redenbacher and Ben and Jerry.

It's an hour before my date with Blake, and I am relaxing at home trying to calm my nerves. My phone rings. I see that it's The World's Best Dating Service. My heart stops. He's cancelled. I knew it. The whole scenario was too good to be true. I am going to be home alone on Valentine's Day. Fantastic.

Hesitantly, I answer the phone. "Hello?"

"Megan. It's Sarah. Hey, I know you are getting ready for your date with Blake, but I have another match I just could not wait to tell you about. This guy is just as great as Blake! You'll really like him!" she says with such confidence.

Let me be the judge of how great he is.

She goes through his laundry list:

Five foot eleven (*Yes . . . and . . .*)

Hispanic. (*Está bien.*)

Has a master's degree. (*I like that.*)

Vacation home in Paris. (*Ooh, la, la . . . oui, s'il vous plait.*)

Looking for a woman with morals and values. (*Check.*)

Divorced. (*Um . . . not so sure about this one.*)

Has custody of a kid. (*Great, that clears things up . . . no, thanks.*)

"Sarah . . ." I say. "He sounds like a really nice man, but I just don't think I am ready to date someone who is divorced with a child."

"Well, other than those two reservations, you'd really be a great fit. You're not willing to give it a try?"

"No, I just don't think I am ready to date a man with a child."

She persists. "I don't think he has full custody."

Sarah, come on, give up. "Regardless, I am not interested."

"He made it really clear that his daughter does not get in the way of his social calendar."

So, now he sounds like a deadbeat dad. You're doing him NO favors, Sarah.

I clear my throat and muster up my most persuasive tone. "Sarah. I am not interested. It is not fair for me to even meet this guy if I am not looking for an instant family. Please, I am not interested."

"So you'll think about it?"

At this point I want to take a page from F-Bomb Bill's book. Instead I respond forcefully but politely.

"Sarah, I need to get ready for my date with Blake. I live in Carson, remember, and it's a long drive to Irvine! I gotta go."

I've got 20 minutes to get ready for my Valentine's showdown.

"ALLISON!" I yell across the condo. "I need some fashion advice . . . I don't want to look like I'm headed to a PTA meeting!"

"I'm coming," she says.

Allison takes one look at outfit number one and says, "NO."

Five outfits later I'm looking hot and feeling hot . . . literally. All those wardrobe changes have worn me out.

11

The Bachelor: Starring Blake

Thanks to Allison, fashion advisor extraordinaire, I'm feeling cute in a white lacy top, black pants, and the highest pair of heels I own. *Thank You, Lord, for making tall men.* While I am not a Valentine's Day hater, I don't love this holiday, and I refuse to wear pink, red or any shade close to either of those.

"What earrings are you going to wear?" Allison asks.

"Who cares? He's not going to even notice," chuckles the confident-but-slightly-bitter-over-this-whole-blind-date-experience brunette in the black stilettos. Allison hands me a pair of crystal chandelier-style earrings. "You never know!" she says with a big smile. I grab my purse and rush out the door.

In the car, my earrings and I begin to doubt our sanity. "What idiot goes on a blind date on Valentine's Day?" I say aloud. I look around. There is no one else in the car. Yes, I am the idiot. And, yes, I am having a conversation with myself. I laugh out loud; it's either that or cry.

Lost in my thoughts, I continue to the restaurant on autopilot. What feels like moments later, I pull into a parking spot. As I get out of my car, I notice a couple of teens walking into the restaurant hand in hand and looking very in love. They stop for a moment and share a sweet kiss. *Jerks.* Though I see this every day, walking the hallways of the high school where I work, I've yet to get used to it. We all remember those "Velcro" couples who seemed to have nothing better to do than make out before school, during passing period, at lunch, after school . . . you get the picture. *Can I PLEASE get a break from the teen make-out sessions?!*

The host tells me that Blake has just checked in and is at the bar. I look toward the bar. *Is every lonely single man at this bar on Valentine's Day?* It's packed. Because I have no idea what Blake looks like, and you can't tell how tall a man is sitting down, I ask the host to point him out. He raises his arm and starts flapping it toward the bar. *Oh, please! Not literally. Discreetly, discreetly.*

"That's him, over there, in the blue-striped shirt."

The host was NOT using his inside voice, and before I knew it, Blake was walking toward me. The voiceover begins . . . "On this season of *The Bachelor* . . ." He fits *The Bachelor* mold impeccably. Tom Brady chin, lean body, well dressed, slightly salt-and-pepper hair (*love it!*) and calm eyes. Calm eyes? Yes. When I saw Blake, my heart stopped racing and I took a deep breath for the first time in the past few hours. I liked what I saw; and assuming the personality and charm matched his appealing appearance, this was going to be a good date. Let's just hope he is not dating five women at one time and handing out roses at the end of the night. *Wait, thanks to the dating service, he might be!*

Blake winks when he sees me, and I break the ice by saying, "Who goes out on a blind date on Valentine's Day?" He smiles and says, "I guess we do!" After seeing Blake, I no longer feel like an idiot. Instead, I think every girl should have a blind date on February 14.

Couples surround our table, but I hardly notice them. In no time at all, Blake and I are comfortable and deep in conversation. Blake tells me that when he suggested we go out on a date on the fourteenth, he had forgotten that it was Valentine's Day. I act surprised, but I'm not. Honestly, if I were a single male, I'd pay no attention to Valentine's Day either. He confesses that not until that morning did he realize what day it was. At that point, he knew it was too late to cancel and too cruel to stand me up. *God bless you, Blake, for saving me from another breakdown and total embarrassment. Stood up on a blind date on Valentine's. You can't script it that pathetic!*

Dinner arrives, and after a few glasses of wine (*Thanks for drinking my share, Blake. No, really, thank you!*), Blake starts to open up the vault and tells me that he's a huge Van Halen fan—so huge that his attendance at concerts is in the double digits. I wanted to ask him if he ever looked like a member of Van Halen. But I did not want to insult him by even suggesting that I could picture him in skintight leather pants with a permed or feathered mullet and an animal print polyester shirt open to the navel. I was just a little tyke when Van Halen was in their heyday and I don't think I could recognize a Van Halen song if I had to. All I know is that they were a hair band of the eighties, and now I assume that most of the members are in rehab.

"So tell me something embarrassing about yourself . . ." Blake says. At that moment, his foot brushes up against my leg. *Footsies? On the first date?*

"Why?" I ask coyly.

"Well, I told you about Van Halen. Now it's your turn." *Um, yeah, Blake, you offered up the info, no one forced you to admit that.* Foot on leg again. I am looking at Blake, expecting a wink or a smile—some signal that yes, he's flirting. Nothing. And then I realize. He's six foot six. His legs have nowhere to go, and mine just happen to be in the way. I slide a bit to the right. (For the record, my leg got no additional action the rest of the night.)

I laugh to hide my nervousness. Following his lead, I share that I have been to three New Kids on the Block concerts. They were cute, semi-talented and cute . . . what teenage girl could resist Joey, Jon, Donnie, Danny and Jordan?! Rest assured this was just a phase. When they came out of retirement last summer, I only attended *one* concert. As boy band followings go, I am not sure you could even consider me a fan.

"Oh, that's nothing, come on, something else."

I am not going to take the bait, Blake.

I will not share the time that I got a shot of painkiller in my butt outside the gates of Pompeii, Italy. Or the time I went on a five-mile run along a crowded running trail with a pair of pink granny panties hanging from the back of my shorts. Not gonna do it!

"Well, I watch *American Idol*," I say sarcastically and with a wink. "But that's not very embarrassing!"

"You are kidding me? That show is ridiculous. Not to mention lame. I'd rather watch karaoke night at a retirement home." Blake's face was very serious and I realize that he actually does find that embarrassing for me.

You're missing out on good, quality entertainment, Blake. I shrug it off and respond with, "It's just research. I need something to talk to my high school students about besides our textbook. That's how I roll." *Good comeback, Megan. Now you SOUND like a high schooler—"That's how I roll." Let's add this very moment to your most embarrassing list.*

In addition to eighties music and *Idol*, we talk about growing up in Orange County, work, exciting trips we've taken and funny dating service experiences. Blake says he has not met any "train wrecks" via The World's Best Dating Service . . . yet. *Let's hope he can still say that after meeting me.*

Before we know it, the restaurant is closing and we realize it's time to go. (*What is it with me closing down restaurants? I am normally in bed by 9:30.*) The date exceeded my expectations. As we get up from the table, Blake says, "By the way, you look great tonight. I especially like your earrings." *Allison, you're my hero.*

Blake walks me to my car and gives me a big hug. I linger for a moment and hope that he might kiss me, and he does . . . on the forehead. *The forehead?! I guess since he's so much taller than me, it was the first thing he hit.* I get in the car and desperately search for a classic rock station on the radio. How perfect would it be for me to end my night with a little Van Halen (not that I would know it was them)? Instead, I get Guns N' Roses' "Every Rose Has Its Thorn." Oh, memories! I think the last time I heard this was slow dancing with Eric Brown in eighth grade. With Axl Rose in the background, my earrings and I recap the night: *What genius goes on a blind date on Valentine's? I do, that's who! Who's the genius now? ME!!!!* I can't help but do a little celebration dance in the Honda.

The next day, Allison and I head out of town for some girl time. The seven hours in the car gave us ample time to recap the date and plan my life with Blake. *I mean, hello?! What could be a more perfect start to a relationship!*

"How did you meet?" people would ask us.

"Oh, you won't believe it. We were set up on a blind date on Valentine's Day, 2008. And we've been together ever since!"

At lunch on Friday, I receive a text from Blake saying he had a great time on the date and hoped to see me the following week. After a fabulous weekend, Allison and I arrive home and it's all I can do to keep myself from calling him right away. *Down, Tiger.* Instead, I decide to order some Van Halen CDs off Amazon. Tuesday night after Bible Study, I see that I have a message from Blake. Allison and I listen to it on speakerphone and I call him back.

The conversation is natural. I tell him about my weekend adventures, including my skid-out on the moped (another embarrassing moment). "I even have the wounds to prove it," I say. *Great, Megan, I'm sure he's really impressed that you don't know how to ride a moped.*

"What were you doing tonight when I called?" he asked.

"Oh, on Tuesday nights I have some friends over to chat and—"

" . . . watch *American Idol*?" he adds with a laugh.

"Very funny. Actually it's a group of people from my church and we get together to talk about a book that we're all reading." I cringe and don't say "Bible Study." What is wrong with that? It's the truth, right? I just fear that it will be a turnoff for Blake. "Right now we're reading a book called *Mere Christianity*. The author is C. S. Lewis."

"Yeah, the guy who wrote *Narnia*."

"Yes, so you have heard of him. Anyhow, this book is about his thoughts on Christianity and his explanations for why he believes in God."

"Huh," Blake says.

"I am really enjoying it, because it has caused me to reevaluate my faith and look at Christianity differently," I say quickly. I wanted to say it. I needed to say it, but it came out as if they were words I just wanted to get out and over with.

Silence on the other end. *Blake, are you there? Tap, tap, "Is this thing on?" I think I've said too much.*

"So you're a Christian." *Is that a statement? A question? A dis? That's not a confident voice. That's a hesitant voice.*

"Yes, it's a big part of my life," I claim with newfound self-confidence.

"Interesting." *Interesting, good? Interesting, bad?*

"What about you? Do you go to church?" I try to sound as casual as possible. I was hesitant to ask, but I don't want to be ashamed or embarrassed about my faith. I want to be confident in what I believe. I *am* confident in what I believe.

"No, I am not religious. I never really think about it. I just think good things happen to good people," he says in a very matter-of-fact voice.

I can feel my palms sweating. It's clear that we're not on the same page. I actually wish we were having this conversation in person because then I could read his body language. I clam up and change the subject.

"Any fun weekend plans?"

"Yeah, I'm really busy. I've got birthday stuff (*What's birthday stuff?*) and I'm helping my sister move. Then Sunday is packed as well."

"Yeah, it does sound like a busy weekend," I say.

"*I'll give you a call next week.*" *Code for: See ya later, Jesus Freak!* Blake never called. I don't know why exactly, but the most likely reason is my faith. I am sad that he didn't give me a chance. But it would have been sadder still had I not been straightforward with him about what is important to me. So to steal a page from Van Halen's book . . . Blake was not "Hot for Teacher." And I was left thinking, "Why Can't This Be Love?"

Any Van Halen fans out there? I've got a few albums I'm looking to get rid of.

As I spent the next few days processing what happened with Blake, I kept asking myself, *Is what I wanted and hoped for in a mate too lofty? Unobtainable? Basically, unrealistic?*

I wrote a few thoughts down to help me process: *There are many things that I am seeking in a mate. You and I both know that the list is significantly shorter than it used to be, but I wonder if it needs to be even shorter? Can I have it all? Can I have a man who is in the world, but not of it? One who is the same at a Bible study, baseball game or a BBQ? Essentially, a man who cares for all different types of people and seeks after You? Will I have to sacrifice attraction or height or common interest in order to be with someone who fits the godly traits that I am looking for? Or will it not feel like a compromise, because we will be deeply in love?*

I want to believe I will have a man of this caliber. Which leads me to ask: Am I a woman who would attract a man of this caliber? If that is the kind of man I want, then that is the kind of woman I need to be.

. . . .

12

Breakdown à la Betty Crocker

I'm fed up. I'm contemplating big-ticket purchases because I'm feeling sorry for myself. I've been shopping for a mate and having zero luck. Now I'm shopping for something I can actually take home with me, something that comes with a robust manual or a guidebook. What do I really want? A new car? An exotic vacation? A Vespa? How about a Vespa purchased in Italy . . . now we're talking!

Reality check: All of the above I cannot afford because I purchased "14 Character Building Experiences" known to some as blind dates. So what can I afford? Food. Yes, food: salty, sweet, deep-fried, packaged—basically anything that calls for butter, chocolate or cheese as the main ingredient. After Bachelor Blake, I decide I'd rather sleep, spend time with my friends, myself or Betty Crocker.

So I eat . . . and I vent. Everyone within earshot learns more about my dating life than they ever wanted to know.

"Did you know that some men tell you they will call and then they don't?" I share this nugget with Michelle like it's an international newsflash.

"Did you know that others make plans for a second date and then cancel and disappear?" I tell my coworker Caroline, expecting surprise, shock even.

"Sounds like he's just not that into you!" she politely replies.

Shut up! Don't tell me the truth. Just tell me what I want to hear.

"Mom, can you believe there are men out there who don't want to date me?!?!" My tone is dripping with disbelief.

"I can't believe it, honey, it's just ridiculous! Their loss," my mom replies. She always knows the right thing to say.

I hate to admit it, but I have reached the dreaded point where all of these disastrous dates have become very personal. The no-call-backs, rejections and cold shoulders have chipped away at my tough J.Crew exterior, and I'm starting to unravel. At the beginning, I shrugged it all off. I put up a brave front. After Blake, blind date number 10, I'm not feeling quite so strong. Defeated is more like it. Commercials make me cry. Teens making out on campus generate a lump in my throat. Every episode of *Oprah* brings me to tears. I need to do something to bring about some healing, and I don't have a cent for therapy.

I'm fortunate to be surrounded by a community of Christians that love me and fight for my heart. First and foremost is my family. I hit the jackpot with my parents, brothers and sisters-in-law. Of course they are not perfect, but I have never doubted their love for me. They are present in every way. This community also includes my Bible study group. This group of 30-something Christians meets weekly under the pretense of studying a book; but now they masquerade as my weekly therapy session. We are each other's counselors and confidants. They want what is best for me. They speak truth into my life, help me keep a healthy perspective and, when necessary, gently put me in my place. These are the type of friends who, at first glance, know when I'm not myself. They know when I need an extra dose of affirmation and affection.

On a Wednesday night in March, I am feeling particularly defeated and arrive at Bible study group on the verge of a breakdown. On my drive there, I had a "come to Jesus" moment in the Honda where everything hit the fan.

"Lord, I am angry. I feel abandoned. I feel overlooked. I feel hopeless. I am trying to trust You, but it is so difficult for me. What is going on with my heart? You know my desire is to meet a godly man, fall in love and start a family. I don't want to wait much longer. My head knows that You can *and will* provide everything I need when I need it, but right now your timeline is confusing. I am 29 . . . 20-freakin'-9! What's the holdup?"

I say all this out loud as if God Almighty is riding shotgun.

I take a deep but staggered breath. At this point, I'm sobbing, so I pull over to the side of the road for my safety and the safety of others and continue talking.

"Lord, right now my biggest fear is me. Have I screwed this up? Have I stepped out of Your will? Am I being punished? I so badly want to please You, but I need to feel You. You are very intangible to me right now. I need to see You in a tangible way."

What I love about my Jesus is that He gets me. He knows my heart. I can say all of this—and worse—and He does not turn away, He welcomes it. Of course my perspective is backwards. I am pointing the finger, blaming Him, writing Him a new one. But He understands and loves me more because I bring my messy self to His feet.

"I am at Cassandra's house, God, but I am not done with You. We will revisit this." I say to the Creator of the Universe like He's a teen that's just been grounded. I walk into the house and everyone is gathered in the kitchen talking, laughing and enjoying freshly made brownies. Not feeling like joining in the fun, I'm noticeably quiet. Everyone knows something is amiss. "Megan, are you doing okay? It looks like you've been crying," Allison says with sincere concern.

That's all it took. I felt I had permission to open the vault and unload. Sobs ensued. Obnoxious. Unsightly. Wretched. I was giving it all I had, putting my whole body into these tears. Everyone got his or her money's worth on *that* night.

I know this expression of emotion is common in most small groups, especially in all-female groups. However, you should know that this small group is coed. Awkward. We have four godly men who love us women well, and thankfully embrace (put up with) our emotions. Tears are often the norm at our meetings. After the sob-fest, I am prayed over, engulfed in their hugs, reminded of God's (and their) love for me and brought to tears of laughter. That night was all about me; a divine appointment with the body of Christ. I was heard by them, and by God (He got a double dose that night!). These 11 people were Christ in the flesh. They *were* my tangibles.

It's getting late and we decide to wrap things up. I'm back in my car and feel like a puppy with my tail between my legs. I want to find a place to hide, too embarrassed to show my face to God. Why do I doubt Him? How can I face the Lord now, after what I said to Him? "Lord, I am sor—" I begin to stammer out. In an indescribable way, I feel silenced. I stop mid sentence. He knows and He forgives. I drive home, hearing Him say, "I love you; I see you; I've got you." Hope returned.

* * * *

The next morning, I realize I never gave the dating service my Blake feedback. It's been over a week, and while they have not called asking for it, I figure I should make the first move. I did face the challenge of politely telling them that Blake seemed great, but when it came to my beliefs, there was a problem. How do I explain that I scared him with my "Jesus talk" and I'm beyond frustrated that none of these so-called "perfect matches" have been a spiritual match? I pull out a yellow legal pad and take a few notes. I'm going to need to get my thoughts together before I make the call. Otherwise, I am confident that the conversation will involve tears. Ugly.

When I call The World's Best Dating Service, I ask for Bridget. She was my first matchmaker and seems to know me the best. I apologize for not having called earlier with my feedback, and I ask if she has a few minutes to chat because I have some concerns about how my experience has been going.

"Of course, Megan. What is going on?" Bridget says.

"Well, first, let me tell you about Blake. We had a really nice date. I felt very comfortable. We had plenty to talk about; he was a gentleman, confident, many of the things that I am looking for. But unfortunately, things did not work out as I had hoped. When I brought up my faith, he bolted."

"That's too bad."

Thanks, Captain Obvious. That's all you got? I feel so much better now. Be nice, Megan. "I have to be honest; this has been an ongoing problem. I was very straightforward with The World's Best when I first signed up for the service. I am looking for a man who shares my faith or is at the very least interested in learning more about my faith. I try not to be overbearing. I try not to have it be one of the first things we talk about, but when the men ask me what I do for fun, or what I am involved in outside of work, the answer includes my church involvement. I find that in most cases, as soon as I bring it up, it's a deal breaker for them or something they are not remotely interested in."

"Interesting. Do you feel like you're a match with these men in other areas?" she asks, clearly trying to look on the bright side and avoid the obvious problem.

You're not getting out of this one, Bridget. Did you not hear what I said? "For the most part the matches have been all right (except F-Bomb Bill), but faith is the most important quality for me; so at the end of the day, the other areas don't hold as much weight."

I pause for a moment, thinking she might respond. Silence. I continue.

"Bridget, I understand that it must be very hard for you to determine how committed a person is to their faith. I know that I took a risk in joining The World's Best Dating Service, because it's not a Christian service. But you clearly stated that you had men who were looking for Christian women and it would not be a problem to find me some great matches. (Bottom lip begins to quiver . . . *pull yourself together, Megan!*)

"Emotionally, this has been a lot harder than I expected. It's not easy being rejected, and I am beginning to think the only reason men don't want to date me is because of my faith. I just wonder if there is anyone out there for me?" My eyes are full of tears.

At this point, I picture Bridget holding the phone six inches from her head, rolling her eyes and making a talking mouth with her hand. I hope I'm not the first woman who has been on the verge of tears on the phone with her. In this case, poor Bridget is both matchmaker and counselor.

"Megan, I think I get it. You want a man who is not afraid to talk about his faith, someone who believes what you do and is willing to share that with you, because it's important to him and important to you."

Amen! I think she gets it!

"Okay, I want you to know that I am committed to finding someone for you," she says. "This must be really frustrating, and I don't want you to leave this experience regretting that you joined. I want you to leave with a man."

Preach it, sister . . . I mean therapist . . . I mean matchmaker!

"Bridget, you get it! I can't tell you how much I appreciate that. Thank you so much!" I say giddily into the phone.

Bridget continues, "I'm going to talk to my supervisor and make sure your next match is a Christian, or at least interested in a woman who does have a faith. I'll even call him and ask him for more info if necessary. I'm going to find you a man that loves God!"

Hallelujah! "Great, I feel much more confident that you'll find someone for me. I have one more question. I seem to meet a lot of men who say they are going to call and then don't. Or plan a second date and then cancel and disappear. I know this might be typical man-behavior (sorry guys, I know us girls can be just as bad), but I am curious if you hear from other women about this same problem."

"Actually, yes, we do get this comment a lot," she says.

Bummer. So I'm not special. *Come on, Megan, for all the reasons to be special, do you really want to be the girl with the least amount of second dates in the service? Leave that title for someone else.*

Bridget goes on, "Oddly enough, we find that some of these men approach their dating experience from a business point of view."

"Really?" I say surprised, because I am.

"Some men want to meet their 14 matches as quickly as possible and then after date 14 they decide who they want to see again and then try to reconnect with those women."

No way! I don't believe it. Not because this approach sounds completely ridiculous to me but because this means one thing . . . Besos Ben might call me back! He might return . . . on a horse, in shiny armor, carrying roses! My heart flutters. *He's just moving through his other matches and then he'll wise up and realize that I, Megan Carson, am the woman of his dreams! Oh, Besos, I'll take you back, horse or not! Height or not! Just hurry . . .*

I snap out of my dream state as Bridget says, "I know it's strange. We try to tell the men that this is not the best approach. Most women don't take too kindly to the idea of a man calling them three months after a date instead of three days after a date."

"Interesting," I reply. "Well, this has been a very helpful conversation, Bridget. Thank you for listening. I just really needed someone to hear me out. Let me know when you have another match for me."

I hang up the phone and head to the fridge. *Um . . . maybe I'd better head to the gym.* I'm running out of "fat" clothes and it's about time I get out of my funk. I've turned the corner and am on the home stretch of dates—11 to 14 are ahead. I can hear my dad saying, "Megan, you gotta get back out there and finish stronger than you started."

Game on!

13

Messy-Hands Mike

. . . .

Post-Blake, it was a good four weeks before the dating service called again. I hardly noticed that so much time had passed. Having gone from someone who never went on dates to a woman who had become a part-time professional at the "first date" (*not something I wanted to go pro in*), it was nice to take a short break from the madness. I assumed the break in the action was due to their need for additional time to search the depths of their dating files for a Christian. I had visions of the matchmakers sitting around their magical matchmaking table, trying to find a date for "The Jesus Freak." I imagine that words like "demanding" and "unrealistic expectations" were thrown around.

Somehow the women came to a consensus, and Mike got the golden ticket. A bilingual lawyer who went to law school on the East Coast, he's described as a "teddy bear" who loves movies and his dog. Oh, and he's Catholic. *Okay, that's better.* I was not sure what to make of the teddy bear description. Is he furry? Soft? Cuddly? Easy to carry around? I feel bad for the poor guy being described as a teddy bear. I guess I'm compassionate because I might, indeed, be described as an old-fashioned Jesus Freak.

Bridget was in charge of this match but was having difficulty finding a time for Mike and I to meet. Apparently, Mike could only meet for lunch, not a drink or dinner. *Strange. The lawyers I know are usually too busy for lunch, but are never too busy for an after-work pick-me-up.* I explain to Bridget that unless Mike is willing to bring lunch to my school and sit with me for 20 minutes while I grade papers and make copies, then this date was not going to happen. As a compromise, Mike agreed to a happy-hour date when school was over for the day.

Bridget selects a restaurant located in a shopping mall. I tried to explain that meeting at a busy mall mid-afternoon is not a good idea—too many potential sightings by friends or students. But she insisted, and I folded. In my mind I could see the painful run-ins: "Oh, who is this guy, Megan?" "Is that Ms. Carson on a date?" "Your mom told me you were back on the market!" "It's about time you found someone!" Thankfully, she chose a mall off the beaten path, so the chances of a run-in were slim.

Unexpectedly, the teddy bear and I meet in the parking lot. Mike appears to be soft and cuddly but not furry, and there's no way I could carry him around. He had a confidence about him that I noticed right away and really liked. Not to mention he's wearing cuff links. *Be still, my beating heart.* I don't know why, but I LOVE cuff links.

The restaurant is empty (*of course it is—it's three o'clock in the afternoon*) and the hostess greets us by name. How is it that people can tell by looking at you that you're on a date? Maybe it's due to the fact that we're the only people in the restaurant *and* the only ones with reservations. In minutes, we're seated with food ordered and Diet Cokes delivered. Then the waiter brings us the restaurant's trademark cornbread. Mike's eyes light up and he gives a little jump. *Is he salivating?* Surprisingly, Mike offers the cornbread to me first and I cut a dainty little piece from the loaf and place it on my bread plate. It's at this point that I realize why Mike offered me the bread first. He wanted the rest for himself.

Over the next 10 minutes, as we wait for our entrées, Mike ate the entire loaf of corn bread . . . with his hands. Never mind a knife or a fork. He just shoved his pudgy little paws right in. Fists full of cornbread, quick dip into the butter, drop in mouth. Repeat. Bread, Butter, Mouth. Repeat . . .

All the while that Mike was eating the cornbread, we were talking . . . about the cornbread. "Isn't this just the best cornbread you've ever tasted?" Mike says with glee. *My bite-size piece is good, but had I had a bit more I might be able to have a more solid opinion.* "Yes, my piece is fine," I say.

"I actually have a funny story about the cornbread," Mike says. "Last year, I was invited to a coworker's house for Thanksgiving dinner. I told him I'd bring my famous cornbread. So the night before, I came here and ordered five loaves to go. My friend still thinks I made it all myself. Genius!"

I laugh. That is pretty smart, actually. I'd do the same thing; but since I am not good with lying, I'm sure I'd confess to having bought the bread.

The waiter stops by with drink refills, and Mike asks for another loaf of corn bread . . . to go.

"I just can't resist. It's great as a late-night snack or for breakfast . . . assuming my dog or my roommates don't get to it first." *Did he say his dog? Does this dog have the ability to open the fridge and get its own food? Impressive.*

"Thanks for being willing to meet me for a late lunch," I say. "I'm sorry I couldn't meet you earlier." *Why did I feel the need to apologize? He is the one who was not willing to meet me after work.*

"No problema, señorita."

Is this what he calls bilingual? That's even basic for Dora the Explorer!

Mike changes the subject to work. "Man, I give you credit for working at a high school. My high school days were . . . well, let's say I've blocked most of those memories out. I got involved in the wrong crowd and spent my senior year working my butt off to try and graduate and get into college."

Sure, blame it on the wrong crowd. Who is this wrong crowd and why is it always their fault? "Apparently, things worked out in the end. You are obviously well-educated and seem like a successful lawyer." I respond, just to give him a bit of an ego boost.

"You got that right!" *No ego boost necessary!*

"So, the dating service mentioned you have Angels season tickets. How long have you had those? Are the seats any good?" Mike asks with such enthusiasm that it's clear he thinks an Angel's game might be in our future.

Umm . . . I wish I had season tickets! "That's funny, I don't have Angels season tickets. Sorry, The World's Best Dating Service misinformed you," I say with a laugh, and then continue, "My dad's company has tickets, though. He says I can have as many tickets as I want if I bring in some business."

Mike does not find this funny. "Bummer, I was hoping we could go to a game."

Bummer, I thought you might like me for me.

Mike continues. "Actually, it's not the first time the dating service has messed things up. They told me one of my matches was Asian. Well, she was not. I was really confused when I showed up to the restaurant expecting an Asian woman and found Anna with red hair and freckles. Definitely not Asian. I actually prefer Asian women, so I was pretty ticked."

Last time I checked, I was not Asian. Two strikes against me. No Angels, no Asian. *How nice of Mike to stick around.*

Is it wrong that I am somewhat comforted to know that The World's Best Dating Service is consistent with their poor matches? I'm not the only one who has been given false information about a match (height and faith being the number-one offender) or set up with someone who was never a good fit from the start. I have no idea how many singletons they have in their database, but I would imagine it's hard to keep everyone straight. I also imagine there are some sympathy dates that take place just so everyone gets their 14. So the question is: *Am I Mike's sympathy date, or is he mine?*

Lunch arrives. I ordered soup and salad—I know, typical girl fare for a date, but that's what I wanted. Mike ordered a big sandwich, half of which is all but falling off his plate. Considering the disaster he made of the cornbread, this sandwich does not stand a chance. *Wait, is he picking up his utensils? Affirmative.* Now that Mike is using his best manners, I am as well. Those country club cotillion lessons were not lost on me!

I'm concentrating so hard on my soup that I almost forget that Mike is there, and then I'm rudely reminded.

Lick.

Lick.

Lick.

Mike has dropped his fork. His hands are covered with the insides of his sandwich. And that sound . . . yes, it's true. He is licking his fingers. Mike finishes his sandwich by gathering the remaining pieces into little bites and popping them in his mouth. With his fingers, of course.

Lick, lick, lick. The check comes. We go Dutch. Cornbread in doggie bag, Mike walks me to my car.

We agree that it was a nice date, but we don't think it's a match. I realize that I learned very little about Mike on this date, but that's okay. Sometimes you just know when someone is not for you.

He does not ask for my number and I don't take it personally; it's not my fault I am not Asian.

It's about four o'clock in the afternoon, and while I wish I could head home, I remember I need to write a test for the next day. I take my normal route back to work, and as I exit the freeway to make a left toward the school, I see fire trucks and police cars surrounding my least favorite store on the block, Robbins Brothers. Robbins Brothers boasts itself to be the "World's

Biggest Engagement Ring Store." More like the world's biggest
reminder that I'm single! The store is large (not Target large, but
larger than most jewelry stores) with white stucco walls and a
Wells Fargo ATM located right near the front door (*cash discount,
perhaps*). Their sign is blue and pink with an oversized neon engagement ring as the focal point. I have the pleasure of driving
past this establishment two times a day, and on this special day,
four stinkin' times.

I hate to admit it, but in a weaker moment, I have thought
of ramming my car into the side of the building. So as I am driving by, and I see all the emergency response personnel, I'm quite
curious. And then I see her. She's sitting on the curb being attended to by a paramedic. She does not look injured, but clearly
confused. And then I see it. Her SUV is wedged into the side of
the building! She drove her car into the side of the engagement
ring store! *Shut up!* I don't know whether to feel sorry for her or
get out of my car and give her a hug and a high five. Was this an
accident? Does she simply hate this place as much as I do, and
she snapped? On behalf of all the women in America who have
thought of going "postal" because they are single, I salute you!

As I continue past the crime scene and pull into the school
parking lot, a dark and depressing thought comes over me. *Just
how close am I to that point?* Could *I* be that woman who is so upset over her single status that she drives her car into the side of
an engagement ring store?

I send an SOS text to Allison:

Please tell me if you think I'm at the point where I would
hurt myself or break the law because I am single. I'm
putting you on "single and psycho" watch. I'll explain
more later.

14

Math-Geek Matt

. . . .

Messy-Hands Mike was my eleventh match. When I first interviewed with The World's Best Dating Service, Jessica assured me that by date number 5 or 6, I would likely meet the man with whom I was most compatible. Not only had those dates come and gone, but I was on the last lap of my 14 dates, and things were only looking worse.

I've always been an introspective person, and of course this journey has been no different. I feel as though I have been detained by dating. I am held hostage by my thoughts of "who" and "when" and "where" and "why not now." What was I doing wrong that I needed to change? What was I doing right that I needed to continue doing? How could I make this work? Maybe the biggest problem was that I was trying too hard. I needed to be myself, give the guys a break and hold this entire experience loosely. I was *not* in control (as much as I was trying to take the reins).

I can't remember how much time had passed between my date with Messy-Hands Mike and my current contestant, Matt. His stats were as follows: number cruncher by day, softball shortstop by night. He had recently moved here from D.C. due to a job transfer. Oh, and he loves music. After 11 dates, the men all start to sound the same, but at least I knew his name and where I was to meet him, so I should be fine.

Up until this point, for most of the dates I dressed kinda business casual. Don't get me wrong, I looked cute, but I was careful not to overdo it or look too "Orange County." That's just not my style . . . I am more sweet than tart, more cute than sexy and more PTA than Miss USA. I wanted to look like me, just kicked up a notch. Allison always did a great job of helping me find the right outfit, and on this night she convinced me to "go all out." I wore more makeup than usual (which is still a "for day look" for most), put on a glittery tank top with a black blazer, my "flaunt-it, work-it, own-it jeans" and gold heels. No need to wear flats because Matt was six foot one. When he arrived in SoCal, he transferred his dating service subscription in the hopes of meeting a California Girl. I am not a typical California Girl; I am actually more D.C. than O.C. *Hope he's not disappointed.*

We were to meet at 7:15. I arrived early and chose to sit in my car and wait. At 7:13, I entered the restaurant and decided to stall another minute, so I head to the bathroom. Clean teeth? Check. All hairs in place? Check. Outfit ready? Check. Here goes. As I stroll through the bar I glance at the TVs. College basketball. *Maybe I should camp out here for a while in the hopes that Matt will want to watch the game?* Instead, I move on to the hostess table.

"Hi, my name is Megan; I have a 7:15 reservation."

Before I know it, I am seated at a table for four, fairly close to the hostess, with a perfect view of the front door. After my wait time with Cheeks, I try to avoid sitting at a table by myself for longer than necessary, but I had gone for a run earlier in the afternoon and really needed some food. I figured I could get started on the breadbasket as I waited for Mike. Every time the door opened I got queasy thinking it might be him. After sighting three potential Mikes, only to see them walk to another table, I realize I've been waiting for a bit and I check my watch . . . 7:23. No Mike. Is there a rule that I can leave after 15 minutes if he is not here by then? You know, like that rule in college that if the professor did not show after 15 minutes you could go back to your dorm and sleep. I mean, study.

Thankfully, I am distracted by the group of people sitting at a long table right in front of me. Three couples with five kids. A big mess and big fun. I know I am staring, but I don't care. In my heart I'd much rather be sitting at their table, happily married with kids. One of the moms catches me staring and gives me a smile that says, "Oh, honey, I hope he comes soon." Yeah, me too. It's 7:29. *I wonder what the score of the game is?*

I look up. The hostess is approaching with a middle-aged man trailing behind. *I thought Matt was 27?* I smile; they pass and stop at the table right behind me. Is this the "Sad and Single" or "Desperate Dating Service" section? Moments later, his dinner partner arrives. Also a middle-aged man. They start talking about work stuff. I check my watch. 7:34. While this still may be the single section, I am now the only representative.

I text Allison. "He's not here yet. I've been sitting by myself for 19 minutes. How long should I wait?"

My phone beeps. Her text reads: "Oh man, that stinks. 7:45 at the latest." *Okay, good. Eleven more minutes and I'm outta here.*

The waiter approaches to see if I am ready to order. "I am actually waiting for someone. Can I just get a Diet Coke and a basket of bread?"

"Is Diet Pepsi okay?" he asks.

No. Actually, it's not. I hate Diet Pepsi. "Yeah, that's fine." I say in a voice that is essentially an audible eye roll.

7:38. *Oh, Lord. Why me? Talk about kicking someone when they're down. I begin to laugh. Am I being punk'd? Ha, ha, very funny! Where are the hidden cameras? No really, where are they?* 7:41.

"Excuse me . . . Miss?" I turn around.

The businessmen have stopped their talk of contracts and budgets and turned their attention toward me.

"I am sorry to bother you. But it's criminal that you are sitting all alone. If he is not here in five minutes, you're joining us."

Now I really feel like I am on a TV show. Did these men just ask me to join them? Yes, they are middle-aged and look like they could be my dad's golf buddies, but they noticed me and want me to join them for dinner. Why don't confident and thoughtful men come in my age bracket? (I know they do, but they must not like my type or live in the area.)

"Thanks, that's really kind of you. I'll give him another minute or two." 7:42.

7:43. Still no Matt. I don't know what to do. Do I leave, hit In-N-Out for a burger on my way home and spend the evening on my couch with a good book? Do I take a risk and join these men and at least redeem the evening? What if Matt shows up and sees me with the other men? Will he join us? Will I want him to join us? Oh, who cares . . . I jump in feet first.

I turn around. "I'd love to join you. Let me just tell the hostess."

I make a beeline for the hostess and then I see him. Faded button-down polo shirt. Khakis with pleats, deck shoes and cell phone clipped to his woven brown belt that has skipped a loop. To top it off it looks like he's stolen Dwight Schrute's glasses from *The Office*. You know, those gold-rimmed beauties. Bless His Heart. He's the before shot of a makeover show. He's a perfect contestant for Beauty and the Geek. Had I moved a minute earlier, I'd be eating with the middle-aged men, not Math-Geek Matt. Unfortunately, he has not made the best first impression. I am not anti-geek . . . I actually find geeks endearing. But I am anti-tardy geek. Matt is officially 30 minutes late. And since I am a girl who views being early as on time, this is off to a rocky start.

Matt and I reach the hostess at the same time. I'm hoping an "I'm sorry" will be the first thing out of his mouth, but instead it's, "Are you Maggie?" *Oh my gosh! It's not him! I am not Maggie!*

The hostess interrupts and says, "Actually, her name is Megan and your reservation was for 7:15. That makes you late."

Woo-hoo-o-o! Step off, Matt! I love that this woman just stood up for me. Maybe she is a jilted single as well and knows the importance of us sticking together. Thank you, sister! Matt follows me back to my table. As I sit down, I quietly say to my middle-aged friends, "Thank you so much for the invitation, but he just arrived." I discreetly point over my shoulder. They wink at me.

Matt apologizes for his tardiness and blames it on traffic. While this is a cliché excuse, it's one that always works in Southern California, because 9 times out of 10 it's true.

"Don't worry, I'll just give you a detention," I fire back.

Matt laughs. *Not surprised that he likes bad jokes. Oh, Megan . . . show some mercy.*

In a few minutes, we order our food.

Matt begins with the standard date questions. Where are you from? What do you do? What's in your CD player?

Mission Viejo.

High school teacher.

Eric Hutchinson, Carrie Underwood, Jonas Brothers (research for my job), a Derek Webb mix (a man who sings about wanting to read the Bible and make out . . . words to live by), Jamie Cullum and Kings of Leon.

Matt tells me he missed life in "The Capitol" as he calls it. He got an A in every math class he's ever taken. He only runs when he is being chased. He's a big Boston Red Sox fan and Ben Affleck is his favorite actor. He takes a weeklong vacation every year, and always the same week.

"Really. That's interesting. Do you go to different places each year or to the same place?" I ask.

"The same place. Either my couch or a sports bar," he says.

Come again? Who vacations to their couch? And unless the sports bar is in an amazing city—

"I'm a huge NCAA basketball fan, and each year I take a week off to watch the first-round games."

Dang, I *should* have camped out at the bar. Matt would have loved to watch the game. Okay, we're finding some common ground here.

Matt also loves eighties music. I like eighties music in small doses. A little Madonna, a little Michael Jackson, a little Abba and I'm a happy camper.

"Now that you know what's in my CD player, what are you listening to right now?" I ask.

"I have an awesome stereo that holds six CDs. I start the morning with Debbie Gibson: Electric Youth. She's the best person to wake up to. Then I have some Bon Jovi, Poison and Queen. I like to rock out sometimes. Then I throw in some Boy George and finish up with Debbie's lesser-known album *Out of the Blue*."

Wow. He was not kidding. He is a huge eighties fan. As much as I wanted to, I did not have the heart to tell Matt that Debbie no longer goes by Debbie. It's now Deborah. A real fan would know that. *Wait, what does that make me?* Then I discover that not only does Matt like bad jokes, but he tells them too.

"Just this morning, when I was getting ready for work, my friend called. I answered the phone and said, 'This better be good, you're taking me away from Debbie Gibson.'"

I laugh. "Ha, ha. Good joke," I say.

"No, I'm serious." He gives me a look that says, "Don't you ever say a bad word about 'My Debbie.'"

How do I recover from that? I've insulted his first love. At this point, I don't really even care, but I give it a shot. "Oh, I know what you mean. When you're really into a song, you just hate to be pulled away."

"Exactly," Matt says with a smile.

Amidst all this, my $8 raviolis arrive and I plow through them. Since Matt is doing most of the talking, he has hardly touched his Everything Pizza (hold the sausage, onions and black olives). He is taking his sweet, sweet time. This would be a prime time for me to do some of the talking, but instead Matt asks if I want to play a game.

"You know I am a huge eighties music fan. (*Yes, this is like the eightieth time you've mentioned it.*) Why don't you hum an eighties song and I'll try to guess it. I'm really good, and I am sure I can guess it in two to three seconds."

"Oh, I am not good at stuff like this. Really, you don't want to play this with me," I say jokingly but with a semi-serious tone.

"Come on, don't be a party pooper," he says.

Did he just call me a "party pooper"? That's it. I'm done. Game over. Literally.

"Sorry, I really don't want to play," I say as straightforwardly as possible. I know I sound apologetic, but I couple it with a glare and he gets the picture.

"Okay, whatever," he says, and returns to his pizza.

Behind me, I hear the businessmen getting up from their table. Matt is preoccupied with his pizza, and as they walk by they mouth "Sorry." *Yeah, me too.* I wink and say, "Thank you."

The check is delivered and Matt says, "Wanna split it?"

Sure, why not? You only made me wait 30 minutes, bored me with your stories about Debbie Gibson, made me feel like an idiot for not laughing at your bad jokes or playing your games. You called me a party pooper and took forever to finish your dinner all the while officially becoming my worst date thus far. Way to go, Matt! Why not split the check? Paying for my $8 ravioli and nasty $3 Diet Pepsi is the least I could do.

Once we have taken care of the check, Matt splits the receipt in half and begins to write down his number. "Seeing as I am new to the area, if you ever want to be my tour guide and show me around, here's my number. Just give me a call. The only days I am not available are those first few days of the NCAA tournament."

I'll be sure to put that on my calendar. In pen.

"Can I get your number?" *No. Absolutely not.* I wish I had said, *"Matt, it's been nice meeting you. Instead of giving you my number, here is the number for AAA. They have great brochures and maps and would do a much better job of introducing you to the area than I ever could. Or better yet, maybe there is a local chapter of the Debbie Gibson fan club you could contact. I'm sure those ladies would love to be your tour guide."*

Instead, I said, "Matt, it's been nice meeting you, but I don't think we're a good fit. Good luck with The World's Best Dating Service."

Math-Geek Matt was not the geek for me.

I head to my car and work to hold back the tears. *Did I really wait 30 minutes for this guy to show up? Yes. But why?* I owed nothing to Matt. Sometimes I am shocked by my perseverance. Maybe you read "perseverance" and think "stupidity." Fair. What I can't understand is why I felt the need to sit there and wait for a stranger in an obviously embarrassing scenario. *Have I lost all common sense?* This is not worth it. I am worth far more than one bad blind date after another. I know I should shake it off and move on, but instead I cry all the way home.

15

Penthouse Pete

Before I went on my date with Math-Geek Matt, I had already secured a date with Pete for Friday night. I had only three days to recover from my unfortunate experience with The Geek, and I feared this would be grossly inadequate. When I arrived home after my date with Matt, Allison was out, and as much as I wanted to talk to someone and debrief, the best thing to do was go to bed. Sleep is the salve that disappointment requires. The next morning—Wednesday, a work/school day—I was not feeling any better. I waited until the last possible moment to get out of bed, even chose to skip a shower in exchange for a few extra minutes under the covers. I did not want to face the day, but I couldn't call in sick because, well, I wasn't sick and I had no sub-plans for my students if I didn't show up. Actually, I did not have plans for when I showed up, either. So, out the door I went, grabbing a Diet Dr. Pepper, a granola bar and a bag of microwave popcorn. Fuel for the day.

I survive a long day at work and decide to go for a walk in the afternoon to clear my head. I throw on workout clothes, grab my iPod and go. It's a beautiful, sunny day, perfectly suited to get my mind off of my situation. I hit play and the first song is about love. Skip. Second one . . . love. Skip. Next one . . . not love, but marriage. Skip. You get the picture. I opt for the sounds of nature. After 30 minutes in the uplifting spring air, I am feeling renewed. I go inside with a fresh attitude, hoping for the best. When Friday arrives, my spirits are up and I optimistically decide that Pete deserves a fair chance.

* * * *

If I were writing a personal ad for Penthouse Pete, it would look something like this:

> Do you like tanning? Real or not-so-real? How about penthouses? Parties that include limos, live music and lemon drop martinis? If so, have I got the man for you!
>
> Meet Pete: Age 34.
>
> Metrosexual money bags with a sexy sports car to match.
>
> Ryan Seacrest look-alike who is concerned about his figure like an obsessive teenage girl.
>
> Penthouse owner, with a $1.2 million second home.
>
> Hobbies include running, sailing and promoting himself.
>
> Interested? Email penthousepete@iloveme.com

How did I find out all of this information, you ask? Over an incredibly long dinner in an uncomfortable, straight-back, modern metal chair.

After my horrible experience of waiting for Math-Geek Matt, I was determined to show up late for this date. Five minutes was not late enough. I waited an additional 10 for Pete to arrive, and when he walked in the door, I clearly saw why he was late. Every hair was in place, every crease perfectly pressed, the eyebrows perfectly plucked; and when he greeted me with a wink and a kiss on the cheek, I could have sworn that he'd practiced it in the mirror more than once. He literally got up close and personal straightaway. *Yuck, Pete! I don't want to smell like your cologne for the rest of the night!*

Pete opened with, "Megan, so great to meet you. What do you want to do? Have dinner or a drink?"

"A drink sounds great," I say, relieved that he gave me the choice.

"Perfect! We'll have dinner at the bar."

Was he planning on drinking his dinner? Bar equals beverages, Pete. I am not here for food, my friend. You're more put together than I am and that is alarming to me. We look over the menu and I decide to order the salmon entrée. I resign myself to the fact that this is now a dinner date, so go big or go home, right?

"Do you work out?" Pete asks. *Pete, are you a bit slow? I am here with you, on a date, remember? There is no need for the cheesy pickup lines.*

"Yes, I do."

Pete looks relieved. "Well, I work out religiously, because I am afraid of getting fat. I really want to look good and have a hot body. I want to order something healthy but have no idea what to order. What'd you decide on?" I was planning on getting salmon and a salad, but now I am considering the Fettuccini Alfredo just to make him want to end the date immediately. Pete would probably think he might gain a pound just sitting next to the creamy sauce and noodles.

"Salmon and a dinner salad," I reply.

"So you are concerned about your figure, too, huh? Salmon is a great choice when you're watching your weight."

Who said anything about watching my weight? It's the most expensive item on the menu; that is the only reason I chose it! Duh!

"I am going to get the salmon," Pete announces, like it was his idea. Orders are placed and Pete scoots his chair a bit closer to mine. "Megan, I have to be honest with you. You are beautiful," he says charmingly as he grabs my hand. "I already know that I want to ask you out again. I've been on so many dates that

I know within about three minutes if there will be a date number two. I've got great news for you (insert wink here), you've passed the three-minute test."

Well, that was easy. My test is a bit more intensive, and thus far, Pete, you're on the fence.

He continues. "So, did they tell you where I live?"

"I think Bridget mentioned Irvine," I say.

"Yes, Irvine is correct, but even Irvine has a hood. Did she tell you where, like exactly?"

I heard you the first time. And, correction, there is no "hood" in Irvine.

"No, she did not," I say.

Pete clears his voice, ready to make an earth-shattering declaration. "Well . . ." Pete pauses for effect, "I live in the penthouse of those new high-rise condos just across the street. You should see my place sometime. It's amazing." Wink.

"Wow! That does sound nice," I say with a tone and just enough excitement to make Pete believe I am impressed.

"Yeah, it's pretty incredible. The penthouse was the only way to go. I mean, why live in an average condo?" *My goodness, Pete. Did you get your degree in social snobbery?* "My decorator is having a blast with the place. We just ordered a handmade rug from Paris. It was such a deal at $8,000."

I almost choke. I look down and adjust the napkin on my lap so Pete does not see me roll my eyes. Pete buys an $8,000 rug from Paris. If I had an $8,000 "rug budget," I'd use it to take a five-star trip to France and then pick up a cheap rug at Target and tell everyone that I bought it in Paris.

"Your penthouse sounds like an awesome place. Tell me more about it. What's the layout like?" I know I will never see it, so I might as well hear about it. And talking about his penthouse obviously makes Pete happy; why not indulge him a bit. Moments later, I am daydreaming, and Pete is deep in Penthouse Land. Out of the corner of my eye I continue to see many attractive men approaching the bar. NCAA basketball strikes again. It's Elite Eight weekend and the game is on the bar's flatscreen.

I'm jolted out of my dream state when Pete says, "So, what does your dad do?"

I am a little surprised to be asked this question. I can't help but think that Pete wants to know what kind of stock I come from. Or what my dowry might include. In biblical times a woman might come into marriage with a few cows, a small plot of land, some jewelry or gold. I guess you could say I have a modern-times dowry. Instead of cows, I come with brothers and a dad who love sports and are "looking for a fourth" on the golf course. My small plot of land is an overpriced condo-*mini*-um in suburbia. My jewelry is a diamond ring that my beloved aunt left me in her will; and my "money" is a teacher's salary that will never exceed five figures. My brothers tease me that I should place an ad that says: have condo, diamond, no debt and golf clubs. Will marry.

On autopilot, I describe my dad's business and then ramble on about my family and my childhood.

The food has not arrived yet, so I excuse myself and head to the bathroom for a break. As I'm walking through the restaurant, I glance over at a large party that looks to be having a great time. I quickly realize this is where all those very attractive basketball fans that I keep spotting in the bar are coming from. And then, high above the other heads in the crowd, I see him. Heartstopping. Breathing escapes me. Feet are no longer moving.

There, 15 feet from me, is the one and only My Mark. He's looking as perfect as I remember him. It's like that scene in a movie when the colors are richer, the lighting is softer and everything is right in the world. Well, not completely right, because I'm here with Penthouse Pete, not My Mark.

Panic. Five-alarm-fire panic! What to do? What to do? *Okay, Megan. Keep walking. To the bathroom, to the bathroom . . .*

Staring at myself in the mirror, I start talking out loud. "How does this happen, Lord? What were You thinking? Putting me in the same restaurant with My Mark, but on a date with Ryan Seacrest's less adorable twin? Evil! This is evil! So, now what do I do?"

I storm out of the bathroom and quickly realize that I have no plan, and Pete is waiting. I start praying for the Rapture. *Come back, Jesus, come back now!* Purposely avoiding My Mark and his party, I take the long way back to my seat. My salmon has arrived and I've never been happier to see food. "Great, our food is here!" I say. Hopefully this will distract my heart for a bit. And now that Pete will be focused on his food, he might talk less. "Did I mention that my penthouse has an awesome kitchen? Sub-zero fridge, wine cooler, double oven." *Of course, back to the penthouse. What else is there to talk about?*

"Wow, with appliances like that you must really love to cook," I say with my mouth half full.

"Actually, not really, but my personal chef said she had to have a fully stocked kitchen. So I delivered."

I wonder what My Mark is doing?

"So, what do you do for fun?" Pete asks. I almost choke on my salmon. Did he just ask me a question? *I'm out of practice with this answering questions thing, Pete. I don't know what to say!*

"I'm really active. I enjoy running—" I hardly get the words out of my mouth before I am interrupted.

"Me too. The most I've run is a 5K, but I run at least five times a week. Like I said, I am afraid of getting fat, so I am crazy about exercise. There is a great trail right behind my penthouse. Sorry I interrupted, what else?"

Sitting up a little straighter on my terribly uncomfortable bar stool, I say, "Well, I run HALF MARATHONS. I've done eight and am training for my ninth right now. They're actually really easy for me . . . I'm pretty much a stud when it comes to running. If you keep working at it, some day you might get to the half marathon distance."

I am not sure if it was the shock of seeing My Mark or the glass of Chardonnay kicking in, but finally (FINALLY!) I said what was on my mind . . . and Pete shut up. *You and your penthouse ain't got nothin' on me!*

The silence was temporary. Pete laughed at my response, and then he started back into his favorite topic . . . himself. "Let me tell you more about my family . . ." Pete took 10 minutes to say the following: mom and dad are divorced, dad lives in Nevada, younger brother is trying to make it in Hollywood and his older brother is a pastor and married with two kids.

"Do you ever visit your dad in Nevada?" I ask.

"Not really. He works for the government doing a lot of undercover work. Secretive stuff, you know, like what you see in the movies (BIG wink from Pete). Mission Impossible, Bourne Identity type of stuff. I actually really can't talk about it. It's all classified information."

Of course your dad is in the CIA. I mean, why not? This is perfect. Maybe he can help me get into the witness protection program, because if I have to suffer through another miserable date, I'll want to change my name, move to an undisclosed location, chop off my hair and start over.

"What about your older brother?" I nonchalantly ask. "You said he's a pastor?"

"Yes. Our whole family is Lutheran," Pete confirms.

"That is great," I say. "Is that still a part of your life today?" I've learned after 10-plus dates that it's best not to bring up religion on the very first date. But Pete opened this door and did not seem phased when I asked him more about his faith. I was pretty confident that I would not see Pete again and that little could redeem this date, so why not talk about religion.

"Yes, my faith is still a large part of my life today."

I lean in . . . *maybe Pete isn't so bad. I mean, he does have a penthouse.*
"I am not really religious anymore, but I am spiritual."
Okay . . . let's unpack this for a moment.
"What do you mean by spiritual?" I inquire.
"I sense that I have been created for a bigger purpose. I think God wants me to change the world through leaving a legacy. I want people to remember me for the impact I make in their lives."
I am buying this logic thus far.
Pete continues. "I mean, I think about my penthouse and how much happiness it has brought me. It's the American Dream, right? Owning your own home. I want other people to have that as well. So I plan on being the next Donald Trump. I want to leave the legacy of big, beautiful, expensive buildings."
That's it. I am waiving the white flag. I surrender; I give up. I am done. I don't know if I am in total disbelief that a man like this exists, or if after NINE setups with The World's Best Dating Service they think that Pete is a perfect match for me. I'm suddenly sick to my stomach and ready to go home. Thankfully, we're done eating, and knowing that Pete would never think of ordering dessert, I lie and tell Pete I have to get up early and need to get going. Pete graciously pays for our meal (with a $100 bill . . . *ooh, I am so impressed, Pete!*) and we head outside toward the valet. As I walk to the door, I take one last, longing look in the direction of My Mark. *Good-bye, My Mark. It's been good, but it's not meant to be.*
Once outside, Pete puts his arm around me and says with such excitement, "Look, you can see my penthouse from here!" I don't look and manage to gracefully pull away from his grip. I hand the valet my ticket, as does Pete.
"So what are you doing this weekend?" I ask, in an attempt to fill the silence; valet wait-time can be so awkward.
"I am headed to Catalina with my uncle, on his yacht. I am really pumped. It will be a perfect opportunity for some tanning." *Did he just say "tanning"?*

"Do you like tanning?" he asks. *Confirmed. He said "tanning."*

"Actually, not really. I like the beach, but I am more of a Frisbee-at-the-beach kind of girl." *I am dying inside . . . it's all I can do to not lash out in hysterical laughter at this point.*

"I hope my car comes first," he says. "I just got my Porsche pimped (exact words) and I'd love for you to see it!"

Penthouse Pete with a Pimped-Out Porsche. Oh, Pete, you just get better and better! And then I see it. Not the Porsche, but my beat-up '99 Honda Accord. How do I know it's mine? It's winking at me. That's right—one headlight is out. *How do you like that, Pete?! You gonna let me set foot in your penthouse now that you know I drive a crappy car? I don't think so! Rethinking that comment about wanting to take me out again?*

I have never been happier to see my Honda. "This is me," I say cheerily, as I take a few quick strides toward my car. Pete is caught off guard, slightly flustered. He manages to escort me to my car and quickly asks for my number. Of course I give him my number, why stop now? I can tell he is trying to stall in hopes that his beloved Porsche might appear. No luck. I've never left a valet station with more speed and agility. *Sorry, Pete.*

Driving home, I compose a hate letter in my head.

Dear The World's Best Dating Service,
    First, you need to change your name. It is misleading.
    Second, you stink. I want my money back.
    Sincerely,
    Megan

P.S. Where do you find these men? Is the circus in town?

16

The State of the Dater

. . . .

As much as I wanted to send The World's Best Dating Service a nasty note expressing the 101 reasons I was fed up with them, disappointed and borderline suicidal because of them, I refrained. Of course my frustrations were entirely their fault (*there is no way I was messing things up, right?*), but I figured I'd better not tick them off before I finished up my subscription. There was no sense in giving Bridget and the team reason to make my next five dates worse than they were already going to be. Gosh, have I become that bitter single girl who is too cynical to believe the remaining guys might be decent matches? *Yes. Absolutely.*

While I did not have the guts to tell the dating service how I really felt, I did need to give them feedback on Matt and Pete. Being honest about these two gems would be no problem. I call, and Monica answers.

"Hi, Monica. It's Megan. I wanted to give you some feedback on Matt and Pete. Do you have a minute?"

"Sure, fire away." *Don't tempt me with verbiage like that.*

"First let me tell you about Matt. He was 30 minutes late. He was nice enough, but had a huge hole to dig himself out of due to his tardiness. I did not find him very interesting, and while he did give me his number, I don't plan on calling him."

"Are you sure it was 30 minutes?" she says.

"I am very sure. I would not make this up."

Monica continues, "I talked to Matt. He admitted he was late, but only by 10 minutes."

"Well, I am sorry, but he's lying. It was 30 long, torturous minutes. I remember every 1,800 seconds of sitting there and waiting for him as a pathetic party of one with the entire restaurant feeling sorry for me. So much so that two total strangers asked me to join them for dinner because I was clearly on the verge of being stood up."

"Okay. What about Pete?"

Really, Monica? That's it? No "I'm sorry," or "Man, that's a bummer, I can't believe he was so late" or "It sounds like you're dealing with some anger issues, maybe you should talk to a professional about this"? All I wanted was a little sympathy. All Monica wanted was to get my feedback and move on. I continue.

"Pete was tolerable, but not really my type. Let's see, how can I say this . . . I think Pete would rather date himself than waste his time with someone else. In his mind, he is the ultimate catch and he worked hard to make sure I realized that."

"So, all in all, the dates were not too bad." *Is she reading from a script? Did she not hear a word I said?*

"I'll call you next week with another match. Have a good day, Megan."

* * * *

It had been nine months since I walked through the doors of The World's Best Dating Service, and in some ways, I hardly recognize the girl who first started out on this escapade. Originally, I joined this service to find The One. Now he seems more elusive than ever. But there's this odd, indescribable and very innocent hope that I continue to have. Subconsciously, there is a battle going on in my heart and mind between reality and fantasy, what is and what I so desperately want.

Reality: I am crazy for subjecting myself to so many dates.

Fantasy: The next date could be The One.

Reality: I'm exhausted and need a blind date sabbatical.

Fantasy: I can't stop now. I might miss him if I do.

Reality: It will happen when the timing is right.

Fantasy: Maybe I can speed things up if I try harder, pray more or do things just so.

While I am very aware that my thinking is twisted and I should be holding this experience loosely, and let God guide me, I am terrified of what He might do. Terrified that He will make me wait. Afraid that I've screwed this entire thing up and that's why I am still single. Frightened that this entire experience will have been a waste because I won't get what I wanted out of it (a mate), but instead what God wants me to have. Why can't I see that what God desires for me is, of course, far better than anything I could hope for myself? Why do I think my God is so small, when in reality He is larger than I could ever imagine? Why would I settle for a mate that would work (basically, silver) when I could have one that God specifically made for me (the finest gold) and then set aside until the time was right for us to meet? I know His ways are higher than my ways, but that does not mean that I understand them. And while I recognize that God offers me unconditional love, I still feel like I have to do right by Him to obtain my heart's desire. What I need is to ask Him to make His desires my desires. I am broken, I am irrational, I am stubborn and I am a work in progress. I am me, but more importantly, I am His.

While my doubts and fears too often take center stage, I have to also admit that I've made significant strides. In this later quarter of my life (we'll just call the second anniversary of my twenty-ninth year), I have become the confident gal I always dreamed of becoming. I am happy in my own skin—I feel strong, courageous and independent. I have embraced my cankles, my tree-trunk legs, my little forehead (which I affectionately call a three-head because it's so small) and my unruly eyebrows. I am a far cry from the pseudo-confident teen who shed many a tear over her looks and personality, or lack thereof. In junior high and high school, I wished I looked a bit more like the cute cheerleader and less like the cute teacher's pet. Now, as a late bloomer, I'm happy with whatever version of cute I currently possess, and I feel great. Finally, at this stage in life, I've embraced my late bloom, and in hindsight, I realize I'd have it no other way.

That's not to say there aren't days when my confident persona is all an act. As confident and "grown up" as I can be, that nervous little girl lies right below the surface, and some days the needy, fragile and weak me appears on the scene—usually after too many glances at magazines like *Marie Claire* and *People* or seeing that couple that's always making out in front of my classroom. (Honestly, don't they have homework they should be doing?) I'm not sure which me is more authentic, Self-Assured Megan or Self-Doubting Megan. Actually, I'd argue a bit of both.

Just when I thought my security could withstand anything, I joined The World's Best Dating Service. Since then, I've questioned my sanity, discovered that my favorite comfort food is salty tortilla chips with a double dose of melted extra sharp cheddar cheese, and that some nights I feel like a sad single sack, and only a pity party, complete with sobbing, will do. Allison holds the Kleenex, and I cry. It has turned out to be quite a routine, definitely a habit I don't want to become too comfortable with. I'd much rather park myself on my familiar blue couch and giddy-as-a-school-girl tell Allie all the details of a great romantic date.

Before my MasterCard registered the purchase of this service, the regrets had set in. Was this a last resort type move that I'd taken prematurely? Maybe I should try Internet dating . . .

again. I now needed both hands and one foot to count the number of couples I knew who met their mate online. Why couldn't it work for me? And I do still have that "You looked better on the Internet" T-shirt—I'd hate for that to go to waste. Dating service and Internet aside, part of me still longs for the old-fashioned set-up. However, at this point, I had tried almost every combination possible. Friend of a friend, single son of a coworker, one of my student's Bible study leaders. The second son of my dad's brother... wait, wouldn't that make us related? For the record, I am not at the point of dating a relative. Arranged marriage? Let's talk.

Maybe if I was not such a sucker, or a people pleaser, I'd not be 15 dates into a year of blind dates—dates that I'd bet money on are worse than yours. But here I am, giving myself daily pep talks that I can do this, enjoy it and be thankful for the whole thing.

So where does this leave me? Prone to be a woman of lists and tallies, I take stock of what I've gained thus far. Here's where I find myself:

A.   More self-aware. I've learned that I often jump into things without really thinking them through. Take for example the paper route I had in elementary school with my brother Keith. Who knew I'd have to give up my Friday afternoons and be bossed around by my older brother?

B.   With a shorter "Negotiable/Non-negotiable" Ideal Man list.

   Negotiable:
   • Golf skills: not required (please don't cut me out of the will, Dad!)
   • Video game skills: now okay (God bless Guitar Hero!)

· Height: can be under six feet but no shorter than five foot nine, and confident enough to let me wear heels.

Non-negotiable:
· Must love God
· Must love me
· Must love dessert

(Of course, there are other things, like thoughtful, respectful, honest, compassionate, patient . . . the same things that most Christian women today have on their list.)

C. With a long list of what I could have used The World's Best Dating Service dollars on:
· Three nights stay at the Four Seasons
· Angels season tickets
· Plastic surgery
· 288 #2 cheeseburger orders at In-N-Out, hold the grilled onions
· 10 gorgeous first-date outfits, with shoes and a matching handbag
· 40 full-body massages

D. With an even longer list of what I could have spent my dating service hours on, according to the following equation:
· "Date Time" = 40 hours
· "Primp Time" = 15 hours
· "Commute Time" = 10 hours
· "In-Tears Time" = about 10 hours total (*Sure, it might have been more or less, but do I, or you, really need to know how much time I wasted crying over these winners? No.*)

Total: 75 hours

37 movies

458 miles run at a 9:30 minute/mile pace

180 commercial-free episodes of *30 Rock* (I love
you, Tina Fey!)

45,000 *American Idol* text votes (assuming I can get
through 10 times in 1 minute)

75 visits to the driving range

So, I press on. And just when I think that The World's Best
Dating Service has gone so far over the edge there's no possibility for redemption, they send me Jon and Ryan.

17

Jon and Ryan to the Rescue... Well, Kinda

Jon was on the upper end of my requested age range, but I'd given up on being picky about age a while ago. As long as he's not old enough to have attended an Elvis concert, been my teacher or fathered one of my students, I'm willing to give him a shot.

I'm one year shy of the big three-o; Jon is one year shy of the big four-o. Still I'm worried that we won't have enough to talk about. Ten years seems like a big age gap, and I am easily intimidated when I'm out with an older man. I have a self-imposed complex about needing to impress older men with clever conversation and my mature allure. Around "older" men I generally talk about current events and fabulous trips I've taken. I comment and inquire on adult topics such as retirement plans, HMOs, PPOs, government legislation and the real estate market. Rather than being wowed by my knowledge of such lofty topics, I imagine most men are bored and think I need to lighten up.

Turns out, the date with Jon was exactly what I needed. He was a complete gentleman. Conversation was smooth. He put me at ease right away and was clearly on the "young" side of 39. Not once did I consider him "over the hill"—I was too distracted by his uncanny resemblance to Lance Armstrong, his funny jokes and thoughtful questions. All in all it proved to be a very normal date. Translation: no curse words and no incredibly odd behavior, conversation topics or jokes. The evening was the perfect mixture of funny stories, comfortable laughter, and get-to-know-you conversation.

We exchanged numbers and chatted on the phone once but did not meet up again. Oddly, I felt fine with that. Going on a fun and casual date meant more to me than feeling like he could be my next relationship. What I needed at this point was *not* to be swept off my feet, but a reminder that kind, funny and wonderfully imperfect gentlemen still exist, and there just might be one out there for me.

After my date with Jon, a small (yet fragile) amount of hope returned to my heart, and each time my phone rang, I was secretly hoping it would be the dating service with my next match. Just three days after my date with Jon, I check my phone after work and was greeted with this delightful message. "Megan, I think I've found the *perfect* match for you." Bridget uses the standard opening line. "I guarantee he will be your best match yet. He runs. He swims. He plays golf and softball. He's tall and thin, with brown hair. He cooks. He cleans. He saves lives and he recycles. He's just, oh, gosh, he's just so perfect for you. I can hardly believe it! *And,* how could I forget, the most important thing— he's a Christian! Really! He said he goes to church every Sunday. *Please* call me back as soon as you get this."

Bridget, you've outdone yourself. This is quite a laundry list of quality traits. Actually it sounds more like my wish list. Where have you been hiding this guy? When and where can I meet him?

I call Bridget immediately and we agree on a local place for dinner on the following Monday night. Bridget tells me Ryan will be coming straight from his spin class . . . one that he takes with his sister. A little sibling time on the exercise bikes . . .

adorable. *I do hope he showers first.* The night before the date, Allie helps me decide on an outfit. Tomorrow will be a busy day and I will need to race home after work, change, freshen up and dash out to meet Ryan in just under 15 minutes. As I am searching through my clothes, Allie sits on my bed looking at a magazine. "Are you nervous about tomorrow?" she asks.

"Not really, I'm more excited than anything else," I yell from the walk-in closet.

"What kind of expectations do you have?"

"Big ones, actually. I mean, *hello!* This guy sounds perfect for me. After so many dates that were memorable for all the wrong reasons, I am really looking forward to going on a date that should be memorable for the right reasons. Come on, he's a Christian *and* he plays golf! The total package," I say with a laugh and stick my head out from the closet door to show her a black silk halter-top.

Allison shakes her head no and says, "You're funny. Just don't hype it up so much that you're certain to be disappointed. I don't want you to get hurt."

"I so appreciate that, friend, but, Allie, could things really get worse? You've had a front-row seat for this train wreck. You've held my box of Kleenex, deciphered my words through uncontrollable sobs, organized an intervention to pull me away from the ice cream and took me to Napa for the weekend with the girls to get me the heck away from this mess. Things can only get better, right?" I end with a question mark in my voice. She raises an eyebrow and lets the question dangle there unanswered. Changing the subject, she tells me to try on a navy shirtdress that she thinks I should wear.

I know she has a point, and yes, I admit my expectations are high, but I'm going to own these high expectations and deal with the broken pieces later if necessary. But of course, that's not going to happen! He very well might be *The One!*

The very next evening, when I arrive at the restaurant, Ryan is already seated. I think I see him in a back corner booth, but I check with the hostess before I walk over. She confirms it's Ryan and divulges that he has been there for 15 minutes. "You're not late," she says in hushed tones, "but he said he was so anxious to meet you that he wanted to get here early." *Love that!*

I walk toward the table and Ryan stands up when he sees me. With a huge grin, he says, "Megan, it's great to meet you," as he pulls out my chair for me to take a seat. I have not seen such a gesture since my days east of the Mississippi. When I was in college, I made sure to surround myself with gentlemen, the kind that always opened doors, chose to walk on the traffic side of the sidewalk and stood up when a lady left or returned to a table. The only thing missing from Ryan was a starched polo shirt and an accent; otherwise, he could easily pass for a frat-tastic Southern boy. *You're off to a very good start, Ryan. I could get used to this.*

Within moments we've established we're beyond pleased to meet one another because we're both Christians and serious about our faith. Ryan has been using the dating service for about 6 months, and I am the first Christian he's met. I can tell he's trying to be nice, but he's definitely not singing the praises of The World's Best Dating Service. It was strangely comforting to know that someone else has had a similar experience; misery does love company.

At the start, Ryan and I had no problem with conversation; but about an hour into the date it suddenly felt as though all the air was sucked out of our corner of the restaurant. When you have elevated expectations for a date, you feel like you're at the starting line of a race, amped up and ready to go. That energy takes you for a bit and then before you know it, you're feeling depleted. You've been sprinting when you should have paced yourself, and you hit the unseen wall.

Ryan and I were unsuccessfully grasping for things to talk about, and the date began to fall flat. I turned my attention to my salad because I wasn't sure what else to ask him. We'd talked about our love of running, his work, my work. His life as a vegetarian, my love of meat; his sweet tooth fought with fruit, my sweet tooth fought with high-calorie desserts. We moved on to travel, family and free time. I'm not sure if he felt it, but it was as if someone had pulled the plug. I've found this to be a problem on other dates as well. What do you do when you just can't think of anything else to say? That's right, you ramble. Before I know it, I'm talking about my students, my grocery list, my roommate and my love of crossword puzzles. Ryan watched me transform from a polite, inquisitive date, asking him all the questions, to one who would not shut up.

The check arrived, but I was too busy talking to notice. Ryan interrupted me and asked if he could buy me dinner. *Of course. How endearing that he deliberately asked me.* The date came to a close and Ryan walked me to my car. "Can I take you out again?" he asked confidently. "I would like that very much," I replied with a smile. Confidence is very attractive in a man, and Ryan had plenty of it. After many men who just went through the motions, I could tell that Ryan really liked me. I had no doubt I would hear from him again.

I get back to my place to find Allie sitting on the couch reading a cookbook (yes, she reads them like novels) and eating a salad. As I am taking in the scene of her comfy pjs, the glorious food on the cover of the cookbook and her dinner, I realize her salad looks very familiar. It has the same ingredients that my salad had . . . the one I had just finished on my date. I glance in the kitchen and see a to-go bag with the name of the restaurant where Ryan and I have just eaten.

Allie is normally very calm and cool, but all of a sudden, she turns red and looks slightly flustered.

"You're home," she says with a look of surprise.

"You're eating the exact same thing I had for dinner," I reply.

"Yeah, well, um . . ."

I am rapidly putting the pieces together in my head. My deliberations are abruptly stopped when I realize that Allie knows that I know. She launches into an explanation.

"I just had to. I am so sorry. I knew you were just up the street, and it was just too tempting to not go up there and spy on you. I figured that I would order some food to go and take a quick peek at him and then be out of there before you saw me; then it occurred to me that you might see me, which, of course, could be disastrous, and I was so relieved when I got there and saw that you had your back to the door and I had a great view of Ryan. But then I realized I wanted a closer look, and since you were near to the bathroom, I decided I needed to go and ended up walking right past you two to get a better look at him. He's rather cute, by the way. He looked at me and we made eye contact, yet I was so afraid that you'd turn around that I abruptly looked away. So wait a few weeks before you bring him around, because by then I won't look familiar to him . . . I am so sorry." Allie finally comes up for air. It does not matter, because I have been shocked into silence. My only response was laughter. Allie was acting like a little kid trying to talk her way out of being grounded. This whole scenario was hysterical to me. Oddly, I felt honored that she cared enough to spy on me. Not many people would take the risk or go to all that trouble. Still laughing, I sit down and fill her in on all the details she missed.

As promised, Ryan called two days later. We talked on the phone for about 20 minutes, and while the conversation was not forced, again, I felt like I was grabbing for things to talk about. I barely knew this man; I should have a thousand questions to ask. Most of our conversation involved making plans for date number two. We agreed on Sunday night—church and dinner afterwards. *Am I really going on a church date? Yes I am! Can I get an Amen?!*

Sunday morning, Ryan calls to remind me about our date that night and we agree to meet at the baptismal. Maybe a dip in the baptismal was just what I needed to cleanse me from all those bad dates and start fresh with Ryan.

I arrive right on time, and Ryan is already waiting for me with notebook and Bible in hand. Both were well-loved (frayed edges, a few tears), a sign that he'd not brought them just to impress me. This happened to be my second time at church that day. After attending in the morning, I had debated calling Ryan to suggest going somewhere else because I feared the topic would be a bit uncomfortable for a date. Marriage? Nope. Sex? No. Singleness? Nada. Circumcision? Yes. That's right, I was about to willingly submit myself to one hour of biblical preaching and teaching on a ritual that made me oh-so-happy to be a woman and made every man squirm. Did I forewarn Ryan? No. Was I nervous? Yes. I did not want to be the one to bring the topic up; I'd rather let the pastor do that.

Round two of the sermon was slightly more painful (ha-ha) than round one, as I observed Ryan (and every other man) struggle to find a comfortable spot in their seat. I was tempted to email the pastor just to let him know that sometimes there are people at church who are on a date and, for the love of all things holy, would he please not mention topics that are uncomfortable—circumcision being on the top of that list.

After church, we went out for dinner and again I felt like a conversation barrier was up. We struggled to get past the basic pleasantries. I was *not* going to ask his thoughts on the sermon, but I could not come up with anything else, so circumcision it was. We laughed about the sermon topic, but it felt like a long dinner as more time was spent in awkward silence than conversation. By the end, I *wanted* to talk about circumcision because at least it was something to talk about. Connecting with someone spiritually is so important, and I knew Ryan and I had that, but if you can't talk to someone for hours and hours, your relationship won't go very far. I was fairly confident that I had no interest in a third date. Sure, it could have been me, but I just believed it should not be this hard to connect to someone. I wanted to give it a few days to make sure I didn't have a change of heart.

No change of heart. Only a lesson of the heart: Ryan was Mr. Right on paper but that doesn't count for much when it comes to living in reality. Just because you match with someone in most areas on a spreadsheet or in theory, if it's not right in person, it's not right. I found myself feeling like I *should* have more excitement toward Ryan. Where had that predate excitement and anticipation gone? Wasn't he everything I was looking for? Was I being too critical, picky or impatient?

In the days after date number two, I kept trying to convince myself that we were a fit, just like I try to convince myself that my favorite high school jeans are not too tight (*I can cover up the fact that I can't button them with a long shirt, right?*). I began to mentally beat myself up for not liking him. After all the time of talking to myself, I kept coming to the same conclusion, and it was only fair to myself, and to Ryan, to move on. So, after four weeks of phone tag (*I know, I let it go on way too long*), I finally told Ryan I did not feel "it." (*I have no idea what the heck "it" is, but neither do you, so don't judge.*)

What a cop-out. Is there a good way to tell someone you're not interested? Is there a good way to say, "I just don't think it's going to work?" Not really. "No spark" or "There's not enough chemistry" is code for "I'm not attracted to you," or in the case of a girl hearing these words, "You're ugly." So I settled with "I'm just not feeling it."

There were some days in the following weeks (normally Saturday nights, home alone) that I regretted having let Ryan go so quickly. Should I have given it more time for us to become comfortable with each other? Should I suggest we try the *friends* route first and forget that we met through a *dating* service? At the end of the day, I was just postponing the inevitable. I had a gut feeling it was not going to work. Call me crazy or overly spiritual, but I trust that if it is meant to be, God will bring him back around.

With some trepidation, I move on. I'm guaranteed three more dates, but who knows, there could be more. (Assuming I want to continue to hit myself over the head with this baseball bat disguised as blind dates.) Oh, joy!

18

The Megan Amendment

I've never thought I'd be a world changer, trendsetter, path blazer—especially in the world of dating. Especially since my first "second date" took place at the ripe young age of 27. (Yes, just a few short years ago.) Yet somehow I managed to single-handedly change a policy at The World's Best Dating Service. Apparently they are as fed up with me as I am with them. It all began with my next phone encounter with match-maker Sarah.

Sarah calls me with information about Miguel. Nothing in his profile really jumped out at me. He basically sounded like every other match I've had except for the fact that he's of a different ethnicity than any of my previous matches. His family is from a Pacific Rim country; I'm from a county on the Pacific . . . it could work!

When Sarah mentioned his name and his ethnicity, I have to admit, I did a double take. When I think Pacific Rim, "Miguel" just doesn't come to mind. And Sarah made no mention of religion. So, I kindly ask if Sarah knows anything about Miguel's religious preferences.

"Well, no," she says hesitantly.

"Does his profile indicate anything about his faith? Maybe that he grew up going to church or attends currently?" I say optimistically.

I hear papers shifting. "Nope, there is no mention of it, but it sounds like you guys could really connect in other areas."

I don't care about "other areas," Sarah, I care about the area in his heart that either loves Jesus or might want to love Him. Has he ever stepped foot in a church? Does Christianity turn him off? Does prayer in his life involve USC winning another bowl game?

"Would you mind calling him to find out? Just ask if he attends church or if he might be interested in learning more about God," I say as politely as possible.

"Unfortunately, Megan, we have a new policy, and we're no longer allowed to ask our clients what their religious commitment is," Sarah says, wincing.

Interesting. What is it called? The Megan Amendment? Or "Just say no to Jesus"? How about the eleventh commandment: Thou shalt ignore the religious preferences of all clients named Megan. So what do I do now? Press on like an idiot? Call my lawyer? Throw in the towel? Instead I ask to speak with Bridget, my religious ally. While I am listening to the maddening "hold music," I have time to formulate my thoughts. This is necessary because I can feel my anger rising. The music comes to an abrupt stop. "Hi, this is Bridget."

Be polite, Megan. I take a deep breath, sensing that I might have a fight on my hands. "Hello there, Bridget. This is Megan Carson. We spoke last month about my matches, particularly finding matches that share my faith."

"Yes, of course, I remember. Have you met Pete yet? I hand selected him for you. He's Lutheran and owns a penthouse. God has been good to him!" *Well, now I know the source of my painful date with Pete. I will try not to hold that against you, Bridget.*

I clear my throat. "Yes, I did meet Pete, but I wanted to talk to you about this new policy that Sarah mentioned. She claims you no longer ask clients about their religious preferences. I was hoping you could explain that to me. I had no idea you had new guidelines."

"Sure. Sarah is new and slightly mistaken." *She had better be mistaken or this is about to get very unpleasant.* "Well, basically, we find that a lot of people don't like to talk about religion or spirituality, and we don't want to force them into sharing about something so intimate. If they bring it up in the interview, that's fine, but otherwise we don't address it. In the long run, we figure it's better for the clients to find that information out for themselves. That leaves the door open to ask questions and discover if you're a match on the religion front at your own pace, when you feel it's best for you."

Translated: You no longer ask clients about their religious preferences.

"So there is no way for me to know if my match is religious unless I ask him myself?"

"Exactly." Clearly Bridget thinks this discussion is over.

"Well, Bridget (*patronizing tone creeping in*), the best time for me to know if I match on the 'religion front,' as you call it, is before I meet a man. However, since it is against the policy of The World's Best Dating Service for me to contact a match *before* we meet, I am potentially wasting dates on men who most likely are not Christians."

"I would not say wasting. Is this not clear to you?" *No, no. Don't you dare question my ability to comprehend crap. I got that taken care of, Bridget. My crap radar is real good and it's off the charts right now.*

"Oh, it's clear. But I think it's ridiculous. I'm sorry to be so candid, but I think it's a waste of my time to have to meet someone in order to find out if he is religious or spiritual, whatever you want to call it. How clear do I have to make it to you that THIS IS THE MOST IMPORTANT THING FOR ME?!"

"Megan, I am really sorry, but there is nothing I can do. It's an executive, company-wide policy. Maybe you should pray that all of your remaining matches are Christian."

Maybe you should pray that I don't sue your employer. I am about to become your personal nightmare, Bridget. What happened? Remem-

ber that heart-to-heart talk we had a few months back? I think your exact words were "I am going to find you a man who loves God." You, Bridget! You were going to find him. Not me. I am paying you to find me a Christian man. Do you realize how much each one of these dates is costing me? I cannot afford to throw that money away on guys who could never be my mate. And forget the theory that this is good practice. Practice should make perfect, right? Well, this is far from perfect and I AM—

I stop my mental venting and let out a long and dramatic sigh, making sure Bridget knows she has one frustrated single woman on the line.

"I am going to transfer you back to Sarah. Have a nice day," Bridget says as though things are peachy. The "hold music" was even more annoying the second time around. Finally, I hear, "Hi, Megan. Okay, so, what else can I tell you about Miguel? Did I mention he has a full head of hair?" she says to seal the deal. "So when are you available?"

19

Miguel the Matador

After my throw-down with Bridget, I have a few days to cool off before I go on my fact-finding mission with Miguel. When Sarah asked where I'd like to meet Miguel, I suggested a fun fusion restaurant I know of. Two days before the date, Sarah calls and says there has been a change of plans. *What now? Did you book Miguel for two dates in one day and now I'm getting bumped?* Looks as though someone (me) might still be a bit angry. Apparently, Miguel does not want to go to the fusion restaurant; he would rather try a new seafood place. That's fine, I like seafood. *If we're going to the restaurant of his choice, he had better pick up the bill.* Snarky single girl is back.

Miguel and I meet on a Monday night, and I've had a really crazy day. My students brought their "*A* game" that day and wore me out with all their questions and excuses. *I don't care if you flat iron your hair each morning, David, you still need to get to school on time.* Yes, some boys now flat iron their hair just like girls. I calmly told David that I, too, flat iron my hair each morning, but I get up a bit earlier to make sure I arrive to work on time. *Teens.*

I pull into the restaurant parking lot a bit frazzled, but looking forward to a good seafood dinner. As I drop my car at the valet (I know, I know, I've become a parking snob), I see Miguel (or someone I think is Miguel) heading toward the front door of the restaurant. I hop out and head toward him.

"Hi . . . Miguel?" I say with some trepidation.

He looks around, like I am talking to someone behind him. There's no one else there. It's just him. I smile. "Oh, I'm sorry, I thought you were someone else."

"No, I'm Miguel," he says point-blank. *Did you have a moment there when you forgot who you were? You acted real surprised when I called out your name, as if no one has called you by your name before.* "Hi, I'm Megan." We shake hands and walk into the restaurant.

Miguel opens the door for me and I check in with the hostess. Soon we are seated and open our massive menus. He's clearly nervous. I can see him wiping his hands on his pants, trying to get rid of the sweat. *Oh, sweaty palms . . . you're such a curse.* He takes a sip of water.

At this point, no words have been exchanged since we've sat down. The waiter comes to take our order and Miguel has quite a few questions about items on the menu. In the end, he orders the Chicken Marsala. *Chicken Marsala? Come again?! Are you really ordering chicken at a seafood restaurant? A seafood restaurant that you specifically wanted to come to? Miguel . . . Miguel . . . Miguel.*

"So how has your day been?" I start with the basics.

"Good. How about yours?"

"Great, cool, good." *What does that mean, Megan?*

"How has your experience with the dating service been?" Miguel inquires. Man, he's wasting no time at all here. Straight to the personal stuff. I guess my next question can be, "When I say the word 'Jesus,' what comes to mind?"

"So far, so good. No train wrecks. It's all good, you know, pretty cool. Sweet."

Megan, can you not put together one intelligent sentence? I mean, like . . . what is like, your problem? Just like, cool down. Just like, relax!

We continue to attempt conversation, but between Miguel's shyness and my inability to form sensible sentences, we're left with very little to talk about. I'm reaching for anything possible.

I have not brought up Jesus yet. *It's all about timing,* I tell myself. *Yes, I fully recognize that is an excuse. Leave me alone.*

"Do you have any pets?" I ask. *Jesus . . . pets . . . don't underestimate my ability to connect the two.* Miguel's eyes light up. "Yes, one dog," he says. Now we're getting somewhere.

"Tell me about her? Him?"

"He's the love of my life . . ." *See? A connection! When Miguel asks me who the love of my life is, I can say, "Jesus!"*

As I learn more about Miguel's relationship with his dog, it becomes very clear that Miguel is a pet lover. This could be a problem. I by no means am a pet hater, but I like pets like I like other people's kids. They are so cute and fun and sweet. At first you can't get enough. Then they get messy and destructive and borderline annoying. Yes, I want kids and look forward to the day when I have my own messy, destructive and annoyingly adorable kid-lets, but I don't see myself having a dog any time soon, and if I ever have a furry friend, I sure won't be calling it the love of my life.

"Wow, he must be a great companion."

Realizing that animals will not be our common ground, I quickly change the subject. "So when you're not working or playing with your dog, what are you doing?" I say in an effort to keep the conversation rolling.

"I like to write. I am actually writing a screenplay about preschoolers who turn into ninjas that try to save the world," he says with total excitement. "I am writing it with a friend, and then we're going to pitch it to every major production company in L.A. Look for it on the big screen in 2015!" Miguel adds with a wink. Miguel seems to have loosened up a bit. Hopefully, I will follow suit.

I didn't want to burst his bubble, but I'm pretty confident that this story has been told with Turtles and artists' names. Twice, I believe. You can add his comment about the screenplay to my list of things that I love and hate about Orange County. While this is not L.A., there are plenty of people in Orange County trying to make it. I don't know if they dream of fame and fortune or really do have a love of acting, writing and starring on (reality) television shows; but regardless of the motive, these L.A. leftovers somehow manage to make their way south while still holding on to their dreams. And since they're not making it in L.A., they take matters into their own hands and create television gold with shows about rich, reckless teens, or homemakers that have too much time and money on their hands. I guess it's the nature of the beast. And while I don't love it, you don't see me picking up and moving to Iowa.

Miguel is feeling more comfortable and says, "So, tell me about yourself." I always find this a difficult request, because I have no idea what the person is really asking me. Just to see if he was listening, I should have thrown in some interesting things like my love of pro-con lists and Scrabble. However, I go with the normal response—teach, eat, work out, hang with friends, church activities, travel. I was hoping he might take the bait and inquire about my church activities, but there were no follow-up questions. Deciding I would rather listen than talk, I ask Miguel, "Do you like traveling?"

"Not really. My last trip was a bust."

"Tell me more . . ."

And thus begins the tale of Miguel the Matador:

Growing up as an only child, Miguel, who loved cartoons, found a kinship with Bugs Bunny and Wile E. Coyote. One of his favorite episodes is when Wile E. becomes a matador. Later in life, when Miguel is a full-grown man, mind you, he decides that he, too, wants to become a matador. Motivated by his childhood memories and aided by modern technology, Miguel does a Google search: Bullfighting lessons + Southern California. Fourty-four-thousand-two-hundred hits later, Miguel has found a bullfighting school worthy of his time and money. He sends in the deposit. Nothing happens. He emails the company, still nothing. Two phone calls later, Miguel is scheduled for his one-day training/bull-fighting package deal and heads to the store to purchase his red cape.

A week later, in the predawn hours, Miguel meets his fellow matadors at an abandoned parking lot just north of the Mexican border. The Master Matador arrives in a beat-up 15-passenger van. A one-hour lesson ensues, and even with limited training the five novice matadors appear to be ready and up for the challenge. The men climb into the van and head across the border. Three hours and one flat tire later, the uneven dusty road they have been traveling on ends at the entrance to a rundown stadium. Upon seeing the bull-fighting arena, Miguel's nerves increase. Will the mini-lesson suffice? When he sees the bulls (though they are just 500-pound babies) his palms start to sweat. He asks the Master Matador for a quick review of their early morning lesson. The Master Matador agrees to demonstrate how to beat the bull. When the demonstration is over, Miguel draws the short straw and must go first.

He walks into the center of the ring, mustering as much confidence as possible. The bull enters and clumsily walks toward him, then stops. Miguel and the bull stare each other down. Traditionally, the bull should charge, but it appears this bull is just as scared as Miguel. They slowly creep toward each other and Miguel begins to wave his cape off to his left side. The bull does not move. Miguel steps closer. More waving. Again, nothing. Finally, Miguel is inches from the bull, waving his cape, and the bull moves . . . not toward the cape, but toward Miguel's face. This is not how the Master Matador had demonstrated.

A few minutes later, and after the dust clears, Miguel comes to. He's bleeding from the nose and mouth, laying face-up on the dirt-covered arena floor. The other novice matadors hover

over him white-faced and visibly scared. Miguel gets up and wipes off the blood with his cape. Apparently the hit knocked all sense out of him and now he will try again to master the bull . . . but this time with a secret weapon. Fresh blood on his cape. Obviously, taking on a bull with a bloody cape will guarantee some attention from this 500-pound baby. On attempt number two, Miguel is successful, though unable to fully enjoy this accomplishment because he's in so much pain. Wanting to look like a macho matador, he tells everyone he is fine and accepts painful high fives and hugs from everyone. The four other bullfighters triumph on their first try. They all walk away with "Master Matador" certificates.

The trip back across the border is excruciating. Miguel claims he's never experienced pain like this before and is so tired when he arrives home that he goes straight to bed. The next morning, after looking in the mirror, Miguel realizes that he might need some medical attention. One trip to the emergency room and two x-rays later, it's determined that the bull won this bullfight. Miguel has a broken nose, fractured cheekbone and mild concussion. And as a result, to this day, he refuses to travel.

"Wow, I don't know what to say. *Olé?*" (*Yes, I am ashamed to admit, I did say that.*) "How are you feeling? You look good."

"Oh, it was three years ago, but I have never traveled since," Miguel says very nonchalantly.

"I am not sure that you can classify that as a trip. I'm thinking it's more like a moment of pure stupidity or lapse of judgment," I say with all sincerity. *Oh, Megan. Not the right thing to say to a man who had his butt kicked by a bull. Have some compassion. You should have stopped at "I don't know what to say." Really, you told him you had nothing to say, but you continued. This is a mistake you might have made on date two or three. But now?! Disappointing.*

"I guess you might be right," Miguel says, slightly hanging his head in embarrassment. This seems like a good stopping point for the date. I have clearly made an idiot of myself and am a bit too stunned to continue. Miguel pays. A very kind gesture toward his not-so-kind date. And he asks for my number. I am taken aback. I had just been so rude to him, and now he wants to take me out again?

Miguel needs to stop in the restroom on our way out. I say a quick, "Nice to meet you," and make a beeline for the valet. I'm really hoping they can get me in my car before he's done in the restroom. I hop in and immediately call the dating service to leave a message. "Sarah, the date with Miguel was memorable. Did you know he's a bullfighter? You might want to add that to his info. I'm afraid there won't be a second date . . . he was a bit shy and I think I said too much."

As evidenced by the bullfighting story, Miguel was a glutton for punishment. He called me the very next day. Allegedly, he so enjoyed our first date (his words, not mine) that he wanted to see me again. I was surprised. Unquestionably, this was due to the mild concussion he suffered three years ago. He was not thinking straight. Did he really want to spend another evening with the girl who had seriously bruised and battered his poor ego with comments like "I think that was a moment of stupidity"? *Miguel, you deserve better, you really do!* I felt like I owed him a second date but was not sure I could face him again. Thankfully, that was a moot point. In the midst of our game of phone tag, Miguel opted to never tag back. I was relieved, but still feel bad. To make it up to him, I'll be sure to see his ninja toddler movie when it hits theaters in 2015. Hopefully, by then I will have some kids of my own and can tell them all about the time their mommy went on a date with the man who wrote the movie.

20

Awkward Alex

It's my opinion that people join dating services for a host of reasons. For some it's an absolute last resort. They've exhausted all their options and feel like there is no other way to meet someone. I wonder if they have tried advertising themselves via junk mail? Infomercial? How about a billboard on Sunset Blvd. or a Super Bowl commercial? What about going door to door as if they were encyclopedia salesmen? It works for the Mormons and Jehovah's Witnesses. When you really think about it, a dating service does not qualify as a last resort; there are much crazier things you could do to find a mate. I keep reminding myself of this on a daily basis. *I am not crazy; I am not crazy; I am not crazy.*

So, why do people join a dating service? There's the obvious reason of looking for a boyfriend or girlfriend or a mate. Or in my case, "If it worked for _____ and _____ (Meggan and Tim, John and Rebecca, Rob and Amy, Sarah and Corey), then maybe it will work for me." There are also the less obvious reasons such as the desire to branch out and meet more people, build confidence (and character), get a few free meals or an ego boost. Thanks to The World's Best Dating Service, now when people ask if I'm dating, I can answer with authority: "I'm going on so many dates, I can't keep up! I'm fighting them off with a stick." Of course you keep the details of how you're meeting these dates to yourself. They don't need to know that you're actually paying to meet these men or women. Minor details, right? In the case of Awkward Alex, I'm convinced he joined The World's Best Dating Service for a few reasons, all of which are of the less obvious kind.

I'm not a superstitious person, but because Alex was date number 13 (not including any of "The Others"), I went into our evening with some trepidation. Honestly, I was expecting the worst, so I implemented a plan to avoid disaster. After Pete and Miguel, I created a new code of conduct for my dates. It would define my behavior. This would be my first opportunity to apply my new rules. If there had been any way I could create a code of conduct for the men, I would have, but I figured there would be no way to enforce it. But if I enforced my *own* code, this might work.

1. Only go on drink or appetizer dates. No more meals. (Not that a meal would take that much longer, but in order to console myself and make it seem like the dates would be shorter, the drink/appetizer option seemed appealing.)
2. Stay positive and be positive. (I realize this might be the biggest challenge.)
3. Don't give out your number just because. (They gotta earn it and deserve it, Megs!)

On my way to the restaurant, I chatted long distance with Leigh and her new love, Dustin. Technically, Leigh was the only one on the phone, but I know Dustin sat close by; and since my voice has one volume (outside, as my parents would call it) I know Dustin heard every word. Thankfully, I could not see his eyes roll and his repeated head shakes through the phone.

Leigh, who I've known for over 10 years, has never been a girl who gushes about guys. She's always had close guy friends, and dated some here and there, but she would rather talk about politics, social issues or Kentucky basketball than talk about the adorable point guard out on the court. While I can hold my own with her on the above topics, I manage to work men into almost every conversation, especially when I am feeling particularly lovesick.

Most of our recent conversations have involved guys because I've been lovesick for . . . well . . . years. What kills me about Leigh and Dustin is how they met. You guessed it—a dating service. On her first try (during a seven-day free trial, no less) Leigh met an educated, handsome, handy, near perfect gentleman. I try not to be bitter, but let me tell you something: I have spent too much money (on the services themselves, the comfort food and the retail therapy) and too much time (getting ready, going on the actual dates, crying over the dates) on my dating life, and what do I have to show for it? Nothing. (*Okay, so not really "nothing" . . . I did get a book deal, but I wanted a husband. H-U-S-B-A-N-D.*)

"So what's this guy like," Leigh asks.

"Um . . . all I remember from his description is that he has a baby face. Oh, and a dog."

"Baby face? I don't think I'd want to be described as having a baby face," says Leigh.

"Yeah, me neither. Did I tell you they describe me as old-fashioned?"

"Oh, in that case, baby face is not that bad," she replies with a laugh.

She has a good point about "baby face." Obviously it's a common descriptor for a newborn, a toddler or a child, but what does it mean when someone in his or her late twenties is described as having a baby face? I'll know in minutes.

I'm early because the only way I can implement my new code is to plant myself at the bar before my date arrives. Regrettably, baby-faced Alex has beaten me to the restaurant and he's waiting patiently with his Arnold Palmer on ice. I walk up to the table and I can tell immediately that he's nervous. That's okay; I am too. Even after all these blind dates, I'm still anxious before I meet my next dud . . . I mean date. I put out my hand and say hello. Alex sets his pen on the table, sets down his BlackBerry and stands up to greet me. Before he stood up he forgot to back away from the table; therefore, the hello was not graceful, but wet. Arnold Palmer is all over the floor and Alex is red. Bless his heart.

Immediately I see that he does indeed have a baby face. Basically, that means he looks like he's about 18, and I begin to worry that those around us will think I am breaking the law by being out with him. Either that or babysitting. I notice that he's made a to-do list on the butcher paper covering our table. There are five perfectly made boxes, one right below the other, with a few notes written next to each box. Some are even checked off. *Hmm, a multitasker! It seems Alex can date and get work done all at the same time!*

"Have you been waiting long?" I ask to break the awkward ice.

Sensing that I've noticed the to-do list, he says, "Just a few minutes. I figured I'd get a few things done while I waited."

Upon closer review, the to-do list includes the following:

- Walk Butterscotch (I learn that this is his beloved cocker spaniel.)
- Call Kim in accounting: 843-2991
- Clean house (Checked off. Apparently he did this earlier in the day.)
- Pay bills
- Reply to email re: presentation (Also checked off thanks to the magic of the BlackBerry.)

I am a huge proponent of lists. I love lists. Grocery lists, Christmas lists, wish lists, to-do lists, what-I-want-in-a-man-but-can't-seem-to-find lists. But I tend to write them on something that is slightly more portable than a six-foot-by-six-foot white butcher paper tablecloth. Different strokes for different folks, right? I don't know, maybe I should try the jumbo-sized list method. Alex might be on to something. I am tempted to reach over and add one more item to Alex's to-do list: Buy note cards or note pad for future to-do lists. Alex catches me eyeing the list.

I smile. Silence. Alex is fidgeting. More silence. "So, have you been here before?" Second attempt at breaking the awkward ice. This is one of the most popular Italian chain restaurants in America, mind you. *What kind of question is this, Megan?*

"Not really, I don't go out much."

Define "much," Alex.

Well, if Alex is not going to talk, I'll take one for the team. Before I can stop myself, I am off. My mouth is running. I just don't do well with awkward silence, and as a result, my awkward social skills come to the surface. Recently, one of my friends told me that it's a major turnoff when a woman talks too much on a first date. But that's what we women do. We talk! It's not nurture; it's nature. We have no choice but to fill silence with sound. Deal with it! I am not sure when Alex (or the waiter) managed to get a word in, but eventually the conversation became two-sided. Unfortunately (or fortunately), I was not the only person with a few less-than-perfect conversational skills.

Alex told me a 15-minute story about his coworker's new tile floor that could have been told in about three minutes. I kid you not. Every two or three sentences were interrupted with this: "I mean like, uh-huh, yeah, like okay." I think the story was about how to faux-finish a tile floor, and had I been paying attention, I might have learned a thing or two, but I was busy counting "likes." Why was I counting? Maybe because I am a high school teacher who wants to rid the world of people who use the word "like" or because it was just so frequent that I could not ignore it. Whatever the reason, I was keyed into this phrase. It was there and frequent and over the top. Now that I think about it, maybe it was payback for my rant about who knows what at the start of our date.

The "likes," Alex and I moved on to topics including his dog and biking and his job. His dog was clearly his best friend and his closest companion. The name Butterscotch was selected because while growing up his dog was named Caramel, and Butterscotch, being similar in color and taste, was the next best thing. Though words were no longer a problem, the conversation with Alex continued with plenty of uncomfortable moments. No amount of Arnold Palmers could chill him out. I hate to admit it, but before long, I began to feel sorry for Alex. I just felt bad that he was so socially awkward. He was clearly uncomfortable, unsure and unprepared for dating.

As I was sitting there, I started to look at Alex from a different perspective and I realized that we had a great deal in common. One of the reasons I had joined The World's Best Dating Service was to meet someone, but also to become more confident as Megan the Dating Machine. Strike that. I just wanted to be Megan the Confident Dater. Alex was date number 13 for me. At this point, I was no longer coming off the bench, I had worked hard and earned my spot as a starter on the team. I was much closer to mastering the fine art of dating. Alex told me that he was three dates into his quest. He was still just warming up. He was a young pup. In hindsight, I can only imagine some of the things I said on my first few dates. I'm sure it was painful to sit across from me as I tried to come up with intelligent things to say.

So, Alex, good for you! Congrats on taking the plunge into the dating world. I give you your props for being willing to risk rejection to meet The One. Raise the roof as you search for a Mrs. Embrace who you are. Because, as my friend Amanda says, "Every pot has a lid." Sometimes it's hard to find the right lid, and you spend time trying on lids that don't fit, but don't worry, she's out there.

21

Sam Obsession

. . . .

I met Sam through one of my friends, Mary. I knew of Mary and her family growing up, but we had only recently reconnected. One day while I was sharing with her about my dating situation, she told me about her friend Sam. He was newly single and someone she thought I would hit it off with. Mary made it very clear that she had never been a matchmaker before and did not want to be held responsible if this turned out to be a disaster, but she was willing to give it a go. You know what my answer was . . . "Why not?"

About two weeks later, Sam called. I was shocked to hear from him. At least once a month (and I am not exaggerating) someone will tell me they have a guy they want me to meet, and I wait and I wait and I wait. Two weeks was record time. *Way to get the job done, Mary!* Sam and I get to talking and he admits that he was hesitant to call. He has never been on a blind date, but since Mary recommended me, he'd give it a shot.

I decided not to share my blind date history (*no need to scare him off before we even meet*) and instead told him I understood his hesitancy. We small-talked for a bit and agreed to meet for a drink the following week. Sam grew up here in Orange County, had spent some time back East and owns his own business. He loves the beach, comes from a great family and is a Christian. And not just because he's an American. He can actually tell me where he goes to church and why he selected that specific church. There were a few silent moments on the phone, but nothing out of the ordinary.

In the days leading up to meeting Sam, I was feeling full of hope and potential. When a friend sets me up, I tend to let myself dream a bit about what could be. I tend to trust my friends more than a dating service. But, in reality, my friends don't necessarily have a better track record than The World's Best Dating Service. Remember Kiddo and Dr. Dirk? Regardless, I dream. I wonder how the first names I've chosen for my kids will sound with his last name? (*Wait, what is his last name?*) What will we do on our second date? How will my parents like him? What will my friends think? How does he feel about golf? On and on and on. Yes, often I set myself up for a broken heart because I am overcome by these Pollyanna-ish thoughts that this will turn out splendidly and I'll finally get the guy.

Once I come out of my sugary sweet coma of idealism, my next thought is this: *Am I so focused on the second date and what could be that I am not working hard enough to actually secure a second date?* Have I become a cocky dater? Have I become the woman who thinks she should get that second date, but in reality, rarely does?

Come on, who wouldn't want to date me? I often ask myself. Apparently, quite a few men. How many dates does it take for Megan to find her mate? Well, at least 17!

Cocky . . . over-confident . . . confused? Maybe all of the above.

The facts do point in that direction. At last count, I've had 17 first dates since September, and only three second dates. And no third dates. Can you really blame me for not going out with some of the men again? Maybe I need to refocus and reassess the riddle behind a first date.

In my mind, a first date really boils down to selling what you have, what you almost have and what you wish you had. First, what you have: wit, humor, intelligence, beauty, confidence. Second, you want to convey that you have ambition and a desire to grow as a person but not talk yourself up too much—basically what I almost have. And third, you have to reveal that you're human but not a high-maintenance hot mess. This requires being slightly exposed by showing that you don't have it all together, and there are things that you still want and need, or things you wish you had. Of course, all of this must be accomplished while not being too serious or too silly, and while looking particularly cute. Not to mention being mysterious enough to leave them wanting more. Dang, this dating thing is hard!

Bottom line: Have I been so focused on a million moments to come that I can't be in the moment on a first date? I'm afraid to admit this might be true.

Back to Sam. We arrive at the crowded restaurant at about the same time. We order a drink and the waitress cards me. Feels good, especially since I am a few years older than Sam. Even though the restaurant is packed (it's a Thursday night . . . the new Friday) we do manage to find a table and settle in for some conversation. We are facing the television in the bar and the Angels game is on. I mention that I like baseball and Sam says he's a big Angels fan. If conversation goes flat we can at least talk baseball and I can wow him with my sports knowledge.

In the appearance and presentation division, Sam is a triple threat. He's stacked in the "man-cessories" department. Cuff links. Monogrammed dress shirt. Fancy watch. New BlackBerry. I love a man with sharp bits and pieces. To me this translates into a man who pays attention to detail. He's going to remember birthdays, anniversaries and favorite ice cream flavors. I like that. The scruffy beard and preppy good looks did not hurt either, and made him a little less metrosexual. I must confess that I have this fascination with businessmen. I especially like their look. Some women like a man in uniform. I do, too . . . the business uniform of a well-fitting suit.

Before long, Sam brings up his ex-girlfriend. Even though this is normally a taboo subject, it does not faze me. It is his ex-girlfriend, and I'd like to believe I am the front-runner to take over the title of new girlfriend. I knew that he was coming off a breakup, but aren't we all? Some are just more recent than others. I tease him that I did some research on Google about what to say and not say on a first date.

"Exes were top of the no-no list, Sam," I say with a laugh. Sam gives me an awkward laugh. Not a "you're funny" laugh. More of a "you're not funny" laugh.

Strike one.

I ask why they broke up. He's a bit evasive, but it boiled down to something about being at different life stages.

"What, was she a lot younger? Age can be a huge issue," I say poignantly.

"Actually, yes, she was younger. But I don't think that was it," Sam says just as poignantly.

Strike two.

"Oh, gosh, I'm sorry, Sam. I didn't mean to make a joke about it."

"Don't worry, I've heard it all. Really, it's for the best," Sam says with a smile. Of course it is—because now you can move on to me!

I breathe a big sigh of relief. I feel really comfortable with Sam and I want a second date (which I now realize is not guaranteed since I've put both feet into my mouth). But I will not go down easy. Sam is so much of what I want (at least according to my list), and I was concerned I would not make a good impression. I am sabotaging the date by trying too hard. If this ship is going to sink, from this view, it was going to be my fault.

Do NOT blow this one, Megan. Be yourself and let Sam see who you really are. Don't overthink it.

One thing I've learned on this blind date escapade is that there are clues or cues that a man might give you on a date to let you know he is interested: a brush of the arm here, a compliment there or a mention of "Let's do that some time." Sam did all of those things. And my little heart crushed harder each time he did. By the end of the night, I was seriously digging this guy. He was right up there with My Mark and Besos Ben. And then he brought up a missions trip he had recently gone on. Are . . . you . . . kidding . . . me! I was buying what he was selling and ready to sign on the dotted line. The date ended with Sam picking up the bill and walking me to my car. He gave me a big hug good-bye and told me he'd call me the following week when he returned from a weekend trip to Colorado.

I left the date feeling very, very, very confident. Sam and Megan. Megan and Sam. *M* and *S*. Sounded perfect to me. For a moment it crossed my mind that Sam might not return this feeling, that he might not be experiencing "Megan Mania" like I was experiencing "Sam Obsession." But I refused to go there. I had no room in my heart for reality. I only had room for Jesus and Sam.

I sent Sam a thank-you text the next morning, letting him know it was good to meet him. I've always assumed that was a good move. There's nothing wrong with letting a guy know you had a nice time on your date, is there? It's not like I professed my love to him.

The problem with sending a text or an email or calling is that now the ball is out of your court and in his. You are now the one waiting. Was that a beep? Do I have a message? Your heart skips a beat any time you hear something even remotely close to your ring tone. And when your phone does ring, and it's not him, your good day has just turned bad. I wait, very impatiently. The three-day window passes. We all know the unwritten but universal law that states men wait three to four days to call a girl they are interested in, right? I start to entertain crazy thoughts such as: *Maybe there is no cell reception in Colorado?* (there is, I've been there); *Did I actually send the text?* (yes, there it sits in my sent box); *Maybe he did not like me?* (Nah . . . it couldn't be that. Don't be silly, Megan.)

Monday comes and I am confident Sam will call.

Tuesday comes and I am confident Sam will call.

Wednesday comes and I am confident Sam will call.

Thursday comes and I am getting nervous and quite disappointed.

Friday comes and I am a wreck. *Congrats, Megan. You've done it again. You got your hopes up and broke your own heart. What are we, four for four now? Right on. What a champ.* I make an emergency call to my girlfriends and we gather after work. I know they will make time to listen to me and encourage me. And they do. Not only did they remind me that my feelings were normal, but in a very loving way they told me that Sam may not be into me, and I need to be okay with that. It was NOT what I wanted to hear, but I knew it was truth. It was a painful conversation but one that needed to take place.

However, I don't give up easily, and I decide to implement Plan B.

Megan, give him a call. Break the rules. Take the next step. What do you have to lose? I tell myself.

I fully believed that Sam did not have the guts to call me (*it had been six days, and by this point he was probably too embarrassed to pick up the phone*), so if he was ever going to meet my parents, I had better give him a call. It was that simple, he's just shy. *No worries, Sam, I am happy to call you.*

"Hi, Sam, it's Megan, from last week. I am really glad I met you (insert awkward laugh) and I think we should go out again (this is going downhill fast). So, if you would like to get together, please give me a call. 949-703-1786. Again, that's 949-703-1786. Bye."

Yes, I left my number two times as if it were an important business call. And it was—the business of my dating life.

I thought that Sam paid attention to details . . . at least his man-cessories told me that. But in the end, the detail that escaped him was that fact that he said he would call, and he never did. Even after I made the desperate call to him a week later. Nothing.

Strike three; I'm out.

22

Lovesick Summer

It had been a long summer. Actually, a very long summer. Due to poor budgeting on my part (*Is it really my fault that Nordstrom has great shoes and J.Crew entices me with their teachers' discount?*), I had resorted to teaching summer school. The cute peep-toe pumps and tweed pants paired with a cashmere cardigan were not worth having to spend 30-plus days with 45 teens in a hot classroom from 7:00 A.M. to 1:00 P.M. And since I was up so early in the morning, my social life took a major hit. I hardly had time for my dates. But somehow I did have time for a few specific events that made me very lovesick.

Summer is wedding season, and I had two on the calendar for the month of August. Even worse, due to 11 failed months of searching for a boyfriend, I would be attending these weddings alone. Thankfully, even under these unfavorable circumstances, my view toward weddings remained unchanged. I love them, I do. (Ha-ha, get it?) Sure, sometimes when I attend a wedding I wish it was *my* day, but most of the time I love being a guest or a bridesmaid and feel honored to celebrate with the couple, their friends and family. However, I don't think weddings love me.

First, I've never been the girl wearing white. Okay, I know my day will come, hopefully sooner than later, but that's not really the issue here. The issue is what I call "Did that really just happen?" moments. I have a long and unfortunate history with such moments. The first wedding in which I was a bridesmaid was outdoors, and midway through the ceremony, a bird pooped on my head. It's really great to be in front of hundreds of people and trying to act calm after you've been pooped on. Little did I know this would be a foreshadowing of even worse wedding experiences.

Being pooped on was quite traumatic, but it did not derail me. After college, I was in a wedding back in Florida. I was more than happy to travel cross-country and stand beside my dear friend on her most important day. Things turned ugly when it was time for the customary bouquet toss. Thanks to this very moment, I now refuse, absolutely refuse, to participate in this rite. And if you attend my wedding, and you are married, it will be you out on the dance floor throwing elbows to catch the bouquet. I will not put my single girlfriends through such an ordeal.

As I made my way to the dance floor, I noticed there were very few women joining me. Actually, no women were joining me. But no worries, I was not alone; I was flanked on both sides by six girls all under the age of 10. There I was, feeling more single than ever and literally standing out from the crowd. Holding back tears, I played along, smiling and laughing as though I were enjoying every moment. The bouquet hit me on the shoulder (mainly because I made no attempt to catch the stupid thing), fell to the floor and was instantly snagged by a five-year-old. The reception's crowd erupted in laughter and I made a beeline for the bathroom where I had a nice little cry, pulled myself together and rejoined the party. Believe it or not, I am still speaking to that friend.

The most recent wedding I participated in was about a week after my date with Sam. It was the wedding of a coworker and my eighth time as a bridesmaid. Both the bride and groom were a few years younger, as was most of the bridal party. I did not know any of the groomsmen; but Sean, the guy I walked down the aisle with, looked familiar (and absolutely adorable in his aviator sunglasses and tux). Over the course of the wedding events, I worked hard to figure out how I knew Sean, but I could not place him. On our way to the reception, I started asking him a few questions to figure out how we might be connected. Upon trying to get to know him better (and working overtime to sweet talk my way to a possible date after the wedding), I had a very strong, very disturbing déjà vu moment as Sean started telling me about a summer camp he attended in high school (10 or so years ago, I assumed) where some people from my small Southern university had worked. I began to think we were on the right track to finding out how I knew Sean. What started out as a small world moment ended with this very unfortunate but very true exchange:

Megan: "Wait . . . what high school did you attend?"

Sean: "San Juan Christian."

Megan: "And when did you graduate?"

Sean: "2003."

Megan: *Okay, so that makes him about seven years younger than me. Still interested.* "That's funny, I used to be a substitute teacher at San Juan Christian—"

Sean interrupted me with this: "Ms. Carson? Oh My Gosh! I totally remember when you subbed for Mr. Roberts. I can't believe I did not recognize you."

I can't believe I am still hoping you might ask for my number. I also can't believe this is really happening to me. I take a moment to compose myself, hoping I will come up with something witty to say. Crickets. More crickets. *Nothing. I've got nothing.* At that point, we start walking into the reception, and it was on with the party. The rest of the night was uncomfortable only because I could not believe I was still hoping he might ask for my number. I know . . . I need help. I left the wedding having given my number to one man . . . someone who needed tutoring for his sixth-grade daughter.

Exactly five days after the wedding, on a beautiful Thursday evening, Allison and the rest of the McCroskey family and I headed to the Greek Theater to see one of the sexiest, most talented singers of standards to walk this earth since Frank Sinatra. Yes, that's right. Gorgeous Canadian crooner Michael Bublé. I love a good concert and I had heard from multiple sources that Michael Bublé puts on one of the best. However, these people who rant and rave about him failed to inform me that attending this concert as a single woman would be disastrous to my emotional health. First, there are very few heterosexual men that are Bublé fans. Gentlemen, you're missing out! And if there are heterosexual men in attendance, they are definitely not single. There is only one reason they are in attendance—they are happily married and their wives dragged them to the concert against their will.

I know, most of you are thinking, *Come, on! Really? You're this pathetic? You'd let a perfectly good evening under the stars, listening to a very sexy man sing very sexy songs make you depressed and lovesick?* Absolutely. You try listening to lyrics like "I get to kiss you, baby, just because I can." Or "You'll never find someone who loves you tender like I do." Painful, I tell you.

In addition to being surrounded by love songs, we were surrounded by lovers. Not since living in Europe had I seen so many intense and very public displays of affection in one place. Between the women who were wearing tight tube tops with "Bublé Babe" written across their chests to couples who could not keep their hands off each other, one very single Megan and equally single Allison could only laugh and make the most of the situation. In the end, the concert was worth it even if the take-home value was feeling lovesick to my stomach and having a strong desire to return someday with the one I love. When we got home that night, I took it upon myself to send out an email to all my single girlfriends with this short warning:

Public Service Announcement
Topic: Love
Title: How to Avoid Being Lovesick. Suggestion #352

Don't ever attend a Michael Bublé concert until you're dating, engaged or married.

Spending two hours listening to a suave Canadian croon about love, love and more love is too much.

Watching couples dance and kiss and canoodle is painful.

It will make you more lovesick than The Notebook. Trust me.

You're welcome.

Yes, I felt beaten by both the wedding and Bublé, but every good fighter gets back into the ring. And because I only had one fight (aka: date) left, I knew what I had to do.

23

Hurricane Taylor

When the end of an adventure draws near, it brings mixed emotions: disappointment, joy, sorrow, gratitude. When the end of a year of blind dates draws to a close, you're not too sad to see it go—it's not typically something you want to hold on to. However, you wish it was ending because you'd found The One, not because your dating service subscription was almost up or you've begun to question the state of your mental health.

The anticipation of the end of my emotional train wreck was more significant than the end itself.

In the days leading up to date 14, I felt conquered. By joining The World's Best Dating Service, I had wanted to claim victory over my dating life, but instead I was defeated by it. To put it bluntly, I felt like a loser. I knew time would reveal the lessons I was to learn from this experience, but in the moments of preparing for my last date, I could not see the lessons through the wreckage. What I could see were wrinkles that had become more defined over the past year, the few extra pounds that were a parting gift from the Blind Date Diet (*staples include lots of high-fat restaurant food and I've-had-a-bad-day-and-deserve-a-treat double scoop ice cream cones*), the zit that had arrived that very morning (*of, course*) and the time on the clock telling me I had to leave now or I was going to be seriously late.

I was stressed over this date and, quite honestly, simply wanted to get it over with. Though I had two months left of my dating service subscription, I was guaranteed 14 dates and that was enough for me. I firmly decided that if date 14 was anything like the majority of my other dates, this would be the last hurrah. I was tired. I needed a break, and two more months of the service was more punishment than I could take.

But why go down easy? Better to go out with a bang, right? *There's the Megan I know and love!*

Selecting my outfit for this date was slightly more difficult because Allison was out of town. I opted for something that normally garnered plenty of compliments—cute white sundress (*Was this too bridal of me?*), strappy heels and a turquoise necklace. I also spent extra time on my hair and makeup. I thought I looked fairly attractive and even took a MySpace-like picture (you know the one: me, a mirror and my camera) before I left to document the occasion. Taylor and I were meeting at my new favorite restaurant, so if nothing else, I was looking forward to a good meal. When did this experience become all about the food? Oh, that's right, when I started meeting men like Kiddo, Math-Geek Matt and Penthouse Pete.

I arrived at the restaurant right on time and managed to sneak into valet parking without having to pay. As I parked my '99 Accord between a Range Rover and a Mercedes CLK, I felt slightly guilty (*Should I pay regardless?*) but I chalked it up to a sign that things might go well this evening. How fitting would it be if the last man I met turned out to be The One I've been waiting for (good things come to those who wait, right)? It might take me awhile to get over the fact that I went through a year of hellish blind dates to find this guy, but I know I would quickly bounce back and move on to my Happily Ever After.

I entered the restaurant and was greeted by a very kind and attentive hostess. Under her breath, she confirmed that I was from the dating service and told me I could pick any open table in the restaurant. *Free Valet + Table of my choice = Great start.* I pause for a moment and she suggests I take a table in the bar in case the date turns bad and then we could just have drinks. *Goodness, what did I do to get this preferential treatment? Who cares? I'll take it.* About five minutes after selecting a table, a tall, well-dressed man approaches me. I immediately stand up to introduce myself.

"Hi, I'm Megan."

He responds by shaking my hand and saying, "Hi, I'm Joe, your waiter."

Super. Way to go, Megan.

Thinking I've just added another story to my list of Most Embarrassing Moments, I awkwardly sink back into my chair.

"Blind date, huh?" the waiter asks. *No, that's how I greet all of my waiters.*

"Yes. Sorry about that," I stammer.

"So, what can I get you to drink?"

"Just a water to start," I say. I am sure my nerves were visible and Joe was thinking, *This girl needs something stronger than water*, but I wanted to wait and see what Taylor was like before I decided if I needed more "courage" or not.

"One water." Joe starts to walk away then pauses and looks back over his shoulder.

"By the way, you look beautiful," he says with a wink.

Woo-hoo, Joe! How nice of you to notice. Thanks to that comment, I start to feel a bit more confident, just as Payton Manning walks into the restaurant.

After checking in with my favorite hostess this look-a-like casually strides directly to my table and I stand up . . . again.

"Hi, I'm Taylor, you must be Megan," he says with an outstretched hand.

I'm a bit flustered, because he is a close copy of the MVP quarterback (and my biggest NFL crush), but I compose myself, smile and say hello.

Once we're both seated, the usual first date small talk starts.

A few moments later, Taylor begins to talk about his stressful day at work. Our pleasant conversation is abruptly interrupted when Taylor says, "Where is the waiter? I need a *%&@# margarita."

I roll my eyes. Thankfully, Taylor has his back turned to me as he cranks his neck to find Joe. What is with these men who cuss? Not in the presence of a lady . . . please! Apparently, the similarities to Payton Manning end with the looks. Southern-boy Payton would not behave this way on a date! I had just recently read in an article that the majority of Americans found cussing offensive. I'm not alone, Taylor. The *majority* of Americans. The F-Bomb record would be broken tonight, I was confident of that. What I did not know was that no word would be safe. Every curse word would be used, at least once.

Okay, Taylor, if you're going to cuss at me all night, then I am going to make you squirm. How do you feel about marriage? Know much about menstrual cycles? Let me tell you all about my ex-boyfriend. How many kids do you want? Being 36 and single, it seems like you're afraid of commitment. Wanna tell me more about that? Do you have a personal relationship with Jesus Christ? Watch out, Taylor. Watch. Out!

Taylor waves down Joe, literally (*Oh, please don't snap your fingers at him*), and orders a margarita. "Make that two," I say as kindly as possible, trying to make up for the fact that Taylor was quite rude. Yes, it has been determined that I am going to need a drink to make it through this date.

Since it's late summer, Taylor begins to tell me about his summer vacation—a family trip to Greece. Sounds great to me—I love my family and I would love to see Greece. He proceeds to explain that this trip was his version of hell. Twenty days in Greece with mom, stepdad, stepbrother, half-sister and 13-year-old niece. Touring all day, getting up early, dirty streets and an "annoying little niece." Actually, he did not call her annoying, he used a more, shall we say, expressive term that I won't repeat.

"Wow, I would have loved to go to Greece with my family. What an awesome opportunity," I say a little too passive-aggressively.

I share that I spent my summer here in Orange County teaching delinquent teens in summer school. I figure Taylor might ask me a few questions about this, but instead he moves on.

"Whatever . . . I'd rather stay in the states even though I've been to all 50 of them. Pretty cool, huh. Besides, the Florida Keys are pretty much the same thing as the Greek Isles."

Now, I don't pretend to be a geography know-it-all, however I do teach that very subject and never in my life have I read or heard the Florida Keys described as comparable to the Greek Isles. I don't have the energy to correct him and, really, I don't care.

"Interesting," I say as our food arrives. I wonder what Joe The Waiter is doing after his shift?

"So back to the fact that I've been to all 50 states." (*Oh, please, I would love to hear more.*) "My parents would pile us into a &%@# station wagon when we were kids and drive us all over the place. It was actually a great way to see the U.S."

"I traveled some growing up as well. We spent a lot of time back East visiting relatives." Again, prime opportunity for Taylor to ask me a question. Nothing.

We're about 20 minutes into the date and I'm fading fast and ready to bail. There are so many "choice" words being said that I have lost count. Somewhere between the cursing I catch things like, "When I was a frat boy . . ." (*What do you mean when? Once a frat boy, always a frat boy, in your case, Taylor*) and "My hot neighbor who cooks for me . . ." (*No comment.*)

Taylor thinks I'm listening, but really I'm not. I'm thinking about what I am going to do that weekend. I have a tennis match planned the next morning, then CPR training and dinner that night with a childhood friend.

"What are your plans for the rest of the weekend?" Taylor asks. How nice, a question. Perfect timing . . . I had just finished planning it in my head.

"Not much, I have CPR training tomorrow and I am playing some tennis. I've been playing a lot of tennis this summer—it's my new favorite game."

"I'm not really into tennis, but I love golf," he says.

I am embarrassed to admit that the Megan of the early dating service days would have found Taylor to be a viable option at this point because he likes golf. It's true. Yet, The New and Improved (yet slightly more jaded) Megan knows that it would take a lot more than golf to get her to change her mind about Taylor. Golf or no golf, I was very uninterested in Taylor. Very uninterested. We are almost finished with dinner; Taylor is now on margarita number two and I've made two trips to the bathroom just because I needed a break from the madness.

"So why did you join the dating service?" he asks.

I am asking myself this very same question. Why did I join this crapshoot? Why did I think this was a good idea? And why didn't someone talk me out of this?

"I joined it to meet The One," I say.

"You're kidding me. You really thought you would meet The One through a dating service? That's pretty naïve."

"Well, then, why did you join?" My tone of voice communicates that I hate Taylor for his previous comment and the way he's treated me this entire evening.

"To meet hot girls who want to have a good time. But I've been pretty disappointed (*that makes two of us*) because most of these women want something serious and some of them have been ugly, so I would not have been interested anyway." At this point, Taylor should have said, "Present company excluded" or "That does not include you." But he didn't. So I did.

"Well, I am certainly not one of those girls. Looks like you've been disappointed once again."

As if nothing ever came out of my mouth, and ignoring my comment altogether, Taylor asks the waiter for the check. Finally, a sign that it's almost over. This storm will pass and Hurricane Taylor will move on having destroyed everything in his path.

"This has been a great date, let's get out of here and go get a drink somewhere." He says this with so much confidence, like he knows I am going to say yes.

Didn't you just have two drinks? And if this is your definition of a great date, then I can see why you're still single!

"No thanks, I'm going to head home."

"Really?"

He's evidently surprised. Strange . . . did he think I was interested? *The waiter asked me more questions tonight than you did, Taylor. The other dates might have fallen all over you, but I am not impressed.*

We say good-bye and he waits at the valet for his car. I sneak over to my Honda and climb in. I pull out of the parking lot and start driving. I have no clue where I am headed; I just drive straight until the street ends in a residential neighborhood. I park my car in front of someone's home and I get out. I begin walking and crying. I am thinking about nothing and everything. I had been on worse dates, and I knew that this was not the last date I'd ever go on. The tears were an outward sign of an inner release. The tears were equal parts relief and hopelessness. As my head began to clear, I couldn't avoid the thoughts that I had wasted so much time and money on this entire experience. And what did I have to show for it? Nothing. Rational Megan stepped in and reminded me that was not entirely true, but for the moment, focusing on the "nothing" was easier than forcing myself to see the "something."

After circling the block a few times, I got back into my car and made my way home. I'd love to say that when I crawled into bed that night I felt the presence of God there with me, telling me not to worry, that everything would be fine. But my room felt empty. My heart felt vacant. In the depths of my heart, I had a sense that God had better things planned for me than enduring a year of blind dates, but assurance of the future was no remedy for the present. I had spent a year putting myself out there, taking risks and picking myself back up after every defeat. I was finally down for the count. The World's Best Dating Service had beaten me, and I was fairly confident there would be no rematch.

Fine Print

. . . .

When I signed my contract with The World's Best Dating Service, there were a few pages of fine print that went along with my signature. Did I read the fine print? Of course not. Do I wish I would have? Well, maybe. Who knows, potentially the fine print would have touched on issues like refunds for rude, late or inconsiderate dates. Maybe the fine print let the customer know that this experience could result in mental, emotional and potential physical harm. All of which I am sure they would not be liable for, and in truth would not have stopped me from signing on the dotted line.

Just like the contract I signed, my story has its own fine print. The fine print is this: I want to fall in love. I want to be married. In my economy, the risk is worth the reward, and obviously I will be deterred by nothing in my drive to become a Mrs. The hope of finding love far surpasses my fear of failure. Relationship, specifically a godly—marriage—relationship, is what I believe I was made for.

Now, I know some of you are thinking this fine print is pretty obvious. So much so that this could be the first clause in my personal dating contract, not buried at the end and written in 10-point font. But here is the kicker, the super-fine print: Even though this desire for a mate is at the core of many of my decisions and guides my emotions, I frequently forget how painful it is to make myself vulnerable to relationship. How could I forget all of the pain that dating has caused me (or I have caused myself as a result of dating)? It's crazy, I know! But it's true! When I go on a date, or try a new dating service (yes, there were others before and have been others since The World's Best Dating Service), I never think about how painful it might . . . scratch that, *will* be. I am consumed with the idea that it could work. I never envision the finish line of my dating service journeys being the same as my starting point. I never want or intend to reclaim my residency in Singleville. I want to move out! This house is on the market, but it seems no matter my efforts (new furniture, fresh paint, clean counters) the market is always down and no one is buying. I remain in this single-family residence.

So, then, I have to ask, What is the problem? Why am I still single?

Is the problem my efforts, my constant looking for a mate? Should I quit trying and stop looking? Well, first, when you are single (and if you live on planet earth), there is no avoiding the fact that you are going to encounter couples, which often makes your singleness more apparent. It forces you to look! You want to be a couple, you want to fit in. "Not looking" is impossible. I'm the child you've told to not touch a hot stove. I'm going to touch it! So when someone tells me to stop looking, I ask if he or she realizes that requires supernatural powers. And that superpower has been lost on me. I'm always looking. I'm not always *longing* for a man but I am always looking!

Should I "Let go and let God"? Well, maybe. I am the first to admit that I could trust God more. I could be more patient, more faithful, more joyful, more self-controlled, more _____ (fill in the blank with whatever fruit of the Spirit you want). But, I also know that God has not given me a mind, intelligence and opportunities just to sit and wait around. He has given me the ability to seek Him for direction and make my own decisions.

This is something I struggle with on a frequent basis. Am I making the wrong decisions and now headed in the wrong direction? Am I messing things up? Have I somehow ruined every one of these 20 dates, and that is why I'm still single? Were my expectations unreasonable? Was I too critical and cynical of the men? Did they never stand a chance? Maybe. I recently expressed these fears to my family. Here is what they told me: Megan, you're delusional and you're giving yourself too much credit. Our omnipotent, omniscient and omnipresent God cannot and will not be thwarted by you.

Okay, should I lower my expectations? Absolutely not! My expectations for dating are high, and why not? I have much to offer, and a man would be fortunate to have me. I have made lists, charts, graphs and diagrams about the man I want. I have pared down my list to the bare necessities. My negotiable list is quite long—golfer, runner, accountant, teacher, blond, bald, it doesn't matter—but my non-negotiable list remains short. I want a man who loves God, others and me. That's it. If he loves God, he *will* be kind and respectful and thoughtful. If he loves others, he *will* be a servant, generous and loyal. If he loves me, he will have a sense of humor (he'll have no choice if he's going to deal with me—after 20 blind dates), be responsible and romantic. I've come to adamantly believe that I can't lose by having a short, well-thought-out list of non-negotiables. I can only lose by compromising those high standards.

Have I learned from my mistakes? Absolutely yes! I will press on, following God's will for my life and growing in my trust of Him. I'll keep hoping for a husband but will ask that God move my heart in the direction He wants it to go, husband or not. I will take myself less seriously. I will look at each date as an opportunity to meet a new person and not as an interview for the future Mr. Megan Carson. I will move on when it does not work, thank God for the chance and for the next potential

match. It will be painful and difficult, but I will not let it con-
sume me or paralyze me. I will not eat my weight in mint chocolate chip ice cream or peanut M&Ms. I will recognize that
sometimes life gets in the way and men don't call for millions
of reasons, not (always) because of something I said or did or
did not do. I will keep a sense of humor in order to keep my
sanity. I will not wait 30 minutes for a date to arrive. I will walk
out of a date if I am being treated rudely. And under no circumstances will I tolerate a man who thinks "effen" is a verb,
adjective and noun.

While I have learned many lessons on this blind date journey, apparently I continue to struggle in one area. I seem to still
be a bit masochistic. It has been almost a year since my last date
with The World's Best Dating Service. Yes, I reached the 14
dates, but I did not use the service for a full year, because I
bailed after my 14 dates, just two months shy of a full year. In
the contract it clearly states that the client gets 14 dates or 12
months, whichever comes later. In my mental calendar, I had
about four weeks left on my subscription. I'd hate to see those
four weeks go to waste . . . and who knows . . . one of those dates
could be The One, right?

Pull out cell phone.

Scroll through numbers.

Select The World's Best Dating Service.

Hit "Call."

"Hi, thank you for calling The World's Best Dating Service."

"Hello, can I speak to Bridget or Sarah, please?"

"I am sorry, neither of them work here any longer. I will
transfer you to Jackie." *I am disappointed that I don't get to chat with
my girls! I've missed my favorite matchmakers!*

"Hi, this is Jackie."

"Hi, Jackie. My name is Megan Carson. I am a client of
The World's Best Dating Service, and currently my subscrip-

tion is on hold. I am ready to reactive my profile and go on a few more dates."

"That is super-fabulous. Give me just a minute to find your file." That oh, so familiar and annoying hold music is back. I wait.

"What did you say your name was again?" Jackie asks.

"Megan Carson."

"Oh, that's the problem. I thought you said Megan Larson. Okay, I'll be right back."

"Megan, I found your file, but it looks like your subscription expired about three months ago."

"Really? I thought for sure I had at least one month left. Can you double-check for me?" *Megan, why are you fighting for this? How sick are you?*

"Yes, the expiration date is right here. May 1. But I can't begin to tell you how perfect your timing is! You're in luck because right now we're offering a discounted renewal rate. Our prices have gone up since you first joined, and even though the discounted price is still a bit more than you originally paid, it's significantly less than what you would pay if you were a first-time customer."

A small wave of disappointment sweeps over me. I don't have the money, and thankfully I have the wherewithal to not go into debt because of The World's Best Dating Service. I guess this really is the end.

"Sounds like a great offer, but I'm not interested," I tell Jackie.

"Really, Megan? This is too good to pass up."

"Well, maybe so, but I am not interested."

She presses on. "If it's a money issue, we offer payment plans."

"Yes, it is pretty expensive. Still, I'm not interested," I say.

"You know, if it means meeting the man of your dreams it might be worth going into debt over."

Click. I hang up on Jackie and immediately delete The World's Best Dating Service from my cell phone.

And the search continues . . .

Epilogue

. . . .

When I started writing about my dates, I found it therapeutic to use humor to describe the men I was meeting. This tactic allowed me to take a fairly painful circumstance and make it bearable. Honestly, it kept me sane. The more I wrote, the better I felt. Until one day I realized that my humor and improved spirits were at the expense of these innocent men. Even in my early days of sharing these stories, I was cautious to "poke fun" at these men, but never attack their character. I have done my best to stay true to that. But, I have to admit; there is part of me that feels guilty to write such negative things about my dates, even though almost all of it is true. So, I've decided to do something that most would think is crazy, but to me feels only fair. I want you to see the other side of the story—to hear from the silent partners of this blind date journey.

So, I present to you blind date number 21, Matt Beans. He was one of "The Others" and is a talented writer in his own right. As further proof that I am a glutton for punishment, I asked him share his perspective on what it was like to go on a date with me, and he was kind enough to say yes. Hey, if you're going to dish it out you have to be able to take it, right? So, here goes . . .

* * * *

When Megan first told me about this book and her blind dating experiment, I was impressed. Going on one blind date is hard enough; going on 20 blind dates sounds like sheer torture. How brave of her to set aside her cynicism 20 times and choose to hope that the next guy will be The One, knowing full well he would likely let her down. And braver still, 20 times she has taken the risk of getting rejected by a stranger and having to ask that horrible, nagging question: "Is something wrong with me?"

In my opinion (and I recognize nobody asked for it), anyone who goes on a blind date deserves a round of applause. And I want to encourage Megan and any woman who can relate to her frustration not to worry over the opinions of guys, especially guys on blind dates. They are all emotional idiots.

I mean that. It's just flawed human nature; all people—men and women—have a bad habit of pursuing unhealthy relationships. So, if a guy shows no interest or doesn't call back, this is not automatically the fault of the girl. Because no matter how confident he may seem, that guy is an emotional idiot. He probably wouldn't know a good romantic opportunity if he called it on the phone and asked it to meet him for a drink at The Cheesecake Factory.

Take me, for example. A little more than a year ago, I went out on a blind date with Megan. (Yes, that Megan—the author of this book.) I thought she was an excellent catch that any guy would be lucky to have. I also believed that both of us enjoyed our evening together and that Megan would've welcomed a follow-up date. But despite all that, I never asked her to go out again.

I know, I know. What's my problem, right? How can I possibly defend such an illogical—nay, stupid—line of reasoning? Well, that's what I mean by emotional idiocy. Let me explain.

I first heard about Megan from my friends Matt and Laura. "The three of us went to school together," Laura told me. "She's super cute and fun. I think you guys would really get along." I trust Laura, so I showed immediate interest. She broke down a checklist of things that made Megan and me compatible.

1. She's a writer. I'm a writer. Check!
2. She's tall. I'm tall. Check!

3. She's pretty. I love pretty. Check!
4. She's athletic. And I've, you know . . . heard of athletics. Close enough!

"Sounds pretty good," I admitted, and Laura pressed the issue. "I'm sure we could arrange an introduction, Matt." Then she raised a dubious eyebrow and added, "Unless the whole Karen-thing is really serious."

Okay. I confess. When I met Megan, I may have been a little out-of-my-mind in love with a young doctor in North Carolina named Karen. She and I met earlier that same year, introduced by a mutual friend. We hit it off right away. And even though we resided on opposite coasts and individually kept two insane schedules, we managed to squeeze in several hours a week to talk on the phone. In addition, I would scrape together airfare and go visit her every couple of months.

Ladies, allow me to let you in on a secret. If you know a guy who drops hundreds of dollars on plane tickets so he can be around you; and if he changes his entire mobile plan to afford talking with you; and if, on the day you turn 26, he has complete strangers call you every 15 minutes and wish you a happy birthday, then take my word for it . . . that guy *likes* you. And what's more, if he claims it's no big deal that while you're dating him you're also dating a bunch of single doctors, well, guess what? That guy is *lying*. He's either lying to you or lying to himself. Or both.

I know what I'm talking about here. I *was* that guy. Karen didn't want a committed relationship, and rather than walk away, I clung to the slightest hope that she might change her mind. It sounds very desperate now, but at the time, I actually thought my choice demonstrated patience, nobility and strength. Meanwhile, her reluctance frustrated me and stressed me out. I didn't sleep well; I dropped weight; I jumped through all sorts of hoops because the idea of losing her completely terrified me.

And yet, on the day I talked to Laura, I must have heard a voice in my conscience scream, "You emotional idiot! Have some dignity and get out of this situation with Karen right now!" Because even though I considered my affection for Karen absolutely serious, I told Laura, "It's no big deal. I would love to meet Megan."

I called Megan up a few days later, and her social skills immediately stood out. Megan knows her way around a conversation; she volunteers personal information, asks thoughtful questions and listens. This takes loads of pressure off any guy. I despise long silences in blind-date scenarios, because I worry the other person is thinking, "Wow, if we don't have anything to talk about already, then we have *no* potential." Long silences send me scrambling for a topic to discuss, until I innocently say something terrible like, "Wow. Your shirt is really green, isn't it?" or "Oh. Your birthday is in February? That's a coincidence. My parents conceived me in February." And trust me, nothing kills a first date like mentioning your parents' sexual history.

As we chatted on the phone, I learned that Megan is a teacher living in "the OC" (yes, I call it "the OC" as well). She also actively participates in her church and has a heart for reaching out to struggling teenagers—all very positive, very likable stuff. Then, I asked her about her writing—a pastime Laura mentioned we both enjoyed. There was a pause on the other line.

"Laura told you about that, huh?" Megan probed. I felt as though I'd disturbed a skeleton in her closet.

"Yeah, why?"

"No. No reason," she reassured me, "I just don't want it to stress you out."

"Stress me out?"

"Oh," she said, suddenly realizing, "she didn't tell you."

"Tell me what?"

"Well . . . it's no big deal . . . but I am writing a book about my blind dates."

I wanted to raise my hand to the waiter and call out, "Check, please!" But given that we hadn't gotten to the date yet, I just sat in silence on the phone.

Of course, Megan was right; the book wasn't a big deal. But the prospect of reading about our date after the fact could be disturbing.

I played it cool with Megan about the book, and she and I made plans to get together. I had a business trip in San Diego coming up and thought it would be a good idea to meet up with her in "the OC" on my way back.

Now, a guy will make his most important date-decisions moments before he leaves his home to pick up the girl. It's that critical time when the forward-thinking individual will make sure to grab his wallet, examine his black shirt for any stray deodorant stains, pick that speck of pepper from his teeth and remove his *Spice Girls Greatest Hits* CD from the car. Before I got on the road to meet Megan, I factored the length of the drive from San Diego to "the OC" against the amount I would sweat in those hours, given that my air conditioning was on the fritz. My quick math informed me that I should make the trip in shorts and a T-shirt and put on my date clothes in the car when I arrived. *Oh, Matt, I* thought to myself, *you're a genius.*

The decision didn't seem quite so clever when I arrived at her condominium complex. Within seconds of parking under the sun without the current of air whipping through the windows, my vehicle became a portable sauna. As I changed in the car seconds later, I was dripping in my own juices. I had to take immediate action. So I made sure the coast was clear and flung open the door. That's when, approaching from that sliver of space in my blind spot, a young woman walked up to find me sopping wet with my pants down around my ankles.

She froze. I froze. And for a split second all I could think was that I was giving Megan the best chapter of her book yet.

As it turns out, the woman was not Megan. Nor was she a resident of the complex. Nor was she someone who knew Megan. I was in the middle of asking her to refrain from mentioning me hanging out half-naked in the parking lot when, without a word, the woman shook her head and walked off. I shrugged and immediately set about pulling on my jeans.

A little later, Megan answered her door with a beautiful white smile. She was tall, slender and athletically built. She welcomed me inside her place and introduced me to her roommate. I got the rundown on how they met, and then Megan and I kicked around some ideas of what we would do. We decided to check out Laguna Beach and grab dinner.

If your only experience of Laguna Beach comes from watching the MTV reality show, you're missing out. It's gorgeous. We walked a path that wound along the cliffs overhanging the ocean and then slowly made our way down to the shore.

She and I conversed on topics ranging from family to college days to professional life and traveling. She spoke with a lot of confidence in the choices she's made, and I got the immediate sense that I was spending the afternoon with a strong individual. Even more important to me, though, I was comforted to discover that Megan's worldview expands far beyond herself. What I mean is that she understands that she's not the center of the universe, so she tends to make the needs of others a high priority. Many of the stories she told about herself involved supporting other people—things like flying to Arizona to help take care of her brother's newborn; mentoring two high school girls who recently got into trouble; going on long trips overseas with her dad to help strengthen their relationship; and volunteering at her church. For me, a broad worldview is the most attractive quality a girl can have.

I am not suggesting that that's the limit of Megan's attractive attributes either. Not nearly. At one point, we were so engaged in our conversation that we lost track of how close we had veered to the shoreline. An aggressive wave bolted up the beach and trampled over our legs up to the knees. I looked to Megan, wondering if she would get upset; instead, she just laughed it off, which told me she did not stress needlessly about things that don't matter.

Around sunset, we ate dinner at a beachside grill. She teased me about putting French fries on my steak salad. I chuckled and told her I learned to do it while visiting my brother at his college near Pittsburgh. "French fries on steak salad is a western Pennsylvania delicacy," I said in my defense. I forced her to take a bite, and she admitted that it was actually really good. So, clearly, she has fine taste in food too.

We pulled up to Megan's condo later that evening, and I walked her to the door. I thanked her for a fantastic evening. No kiss. Just a friendly hug seemed most appropriate, and we agreed we would get in touch soon. I strolled across the parking lot and got into my car. Within a few seconds, I was cruising on the 405 Freeway with the windows down and the cool evening gliding against my cheek. I smiled to myself, thinking what a good time I'd had.

And yet, my fingers were already opening my phone to call Karen.

I guess when you're an emotional idiot you just have to learn some lessons the hard way. Karen and I played at romance for a few more months. But with each passing day she grew more and more distant, which prompted me to work harder and harder to keep her attention. Then, in the winter, I came down with a bad case of writer's block and, a little later, I wrecked my car. The combined stress forced me to relieve pressure elsewhere in my life by doing something I should've done a long time before. I phoned Karen and, through a big lump in my throat, I asked her if she wanted to call it quits. She did.

See what Megan was up against? The chances that, in one night, she could impress me enough to make me forget about Karen were 100 to 1. Maybe 1,000 to 1. By that account, 20 dates are a drop in the bucket. But these are the odds of anybody finding The One on a blind date, because none of us meet objective, unbiased men and women. We meet emotional idiots—all with their own history of insecurities and flaws and hurts.

Despite my emotional idiocy, I did think Megan and I had limited potential as a couple. We didn't share the same sense of humor, for one. Plus, it's not like Los Angeles (where I live) and "the OC" (where she lives) sit within a short drive of one another. And regardless of our shared interest in writing, our pursuits don't match up very well. So, I'm not saying we would be happily married now if only I had woken up and set myself free of Karen. But that's not the point. The point is that blind dating—no, dating, in general—is very, very difficult for everyone. So, when we hit a string of bad luck, we need to cut ourselves a break and remember that the outcome is mostly out of our control.

Oh, one last thing, Megan: In order to write this chapter, I had to assume I was one of the guys you wanted to go out with again, which probably seems arrogant. But consider the alternative. Otherwise, I had to view myself as one of those goofballs your readers are laughing at right now. And I just couldn't bear to do that. Hope you understand. Thanks, kiddo!

—Matt Beans

Last Word

PhD in dating: ☑
Thicker skin: ☑
A deeper faith: ☑
Increased confidence: ☑
Contentment and joy: ☑
Happy ending: ☑
Relationship with a man who loves her *and* her God: ☐

Yep, that last box is still empty. I'm currently a resident of Singleville. And while I look forward to moving out, I absolutely got my happy ending. *How is that possible, Megan? You're still single!* All it took was for me to change my definition of a "happy ending." I have found contentment and joy in being exactly where God wants me to be, and that is what makes me happy.

Acknowledgments

God, thank You for showing me gold and not giving me silver. You have saved me by Your grace. You do not abandon the works of Your hands.

Dad, you have set the bar high. Through your love, provision and service to our family, I see the qualities I want in a man. You have loved me well—and you'll always be my favorite dance partner. Mom, you are my champion. You have raised me to be a confident woman and lead by example. I have never doubted how much you love me and how proud you are of me.

Keith and Drew, I am honored and proud to have you as brothers. Tracy and Jenny, you have made our family more complete. I look forward to all the years to come of growing, laughing and doing life together. Owen and William, you are pure joy in my life. Aunt Lee, I miss you every day and smile knowing you would be so proud of me.

Allison, you are wise beyond your years. Elise, you always reminded me that God was in control. Erin, you asked the hard questions. Jennifer, your phone calls were my lifelines. Sharon, you encouraged me to embrace my story and helped me improve it. Mary Anne, you reminded me to take God seriously and lighten up. Leigh and Amanda, you are my friends for a lifetime. Michelle, you get me.

To my small group and the girls at the lunch table, you've held my hand (in some cases, literally) through this whole process of dating and writing. You've shared in my joys and encouraged me in my sorrows. Thank you.

To my agent, Bucky Rosenbaum, thank you for guiding me though this process and treating me more like a daughter than a client. To Steve Lawson and everyone at Regal, thank you for taking a chance on a first-time author with such a crazy story to tell.

Finally, to the men in this story, thank you for giving me fantastic material and teaching me some invaluable lessons. I am glad we met, but I hope to never see you again.

Author Contact

· ·

To book Megan for an event, ask her a question or
see if she is available Friday night, contact her at:

www.megancarson.com